PROGRESSIVE
AIKIDO

PROGRESSIVE AIKIDO
The Essential Elements

Moriteru Ueshiba

Translated by John Stevens

KODANSHA INTERNATIONAL
Tokyo · New York · London

Contact information for the Aikikai Foundation is as follows:

Aikido World Headquarters
Aikikai Foundation
17–18 Wakamatsu-cho
Shinjuku-ku
Tokyo 162–0056
Japan
Tel: 81–(0)3–3203–9236
Fax: 81–(0)3–3204–8145
Website: www.aikikai.or.jp
E-mail: aikido@aikikai.or.jp

Photographs by Kyuzo Akashi.

Waza techniques are demonstrated by the author as *tori* and Takeshi Kanazawa, Yoshinobu Irie, and Toshio Suzuki as *uke*.

Distributed in the United States by Kodansha America Inc., and in the United Kingdom and continental Europe by Kodansha Europe Ltd.

Published by Kodansha International Ltd., 17–14 Otowa 1-chome, Bunkyo-ku, Tokyo 112–8652, and Kodansha America, Inc.

Copyright © 2005 by Moriteru Ueshiba and Kodansha International Ltd. Translation copyright © 2005 by John Stevens.
All rights reserved. Printed in Japan.
ISBN 978-4-7700-2172-4

First edition, 2005
15 14 13 12 11 10 09 08 07   10 9 8 7 6 5 4 3 2

www.kodansha-intl.com

PREFACE

When people begin the practice of Aikido, the first question they usually ask is: "During practice, what is the most important element to learn first from the instructor?"

In Aikido training, the first things we learn are the *hanmi* stance, *irimi*, *tenkan*, and how to develop *kokyu* power. In all these Aikido techniques, the most important and fundamental element is proper movement. Making proper movement your base, you will be able to master fundamental techniques, advanced techniques, and applied techniques. In other words, from the beginning, a thorough step-by-step approach is necessary. Master the basics and your skill will naturally improve in training.

This manual is based on a systematic, step-by-step approach using proper movement to train in fundamental, essential, and applied techniques in the correct order. My hope is that the illustrations and explanations in this manual will prove useful for both beginners and senior instructors in Aikido.

Beginner students should absorb as much as they can from their instructors; senior practitioners should retain the desire to improve. This is the meaning of *keiko*, "training," in Aikido. If this manual helps the many practitioners of Aikido to improve in any way, whatever their level, I will be very pleased.

Moriteru Ueshiba

CONTENTS

PREFACE   6

CHAPTER 1   INTRODUCTION TO AIKIDO PRINCIPLES   11

WHAT IS AIKIDO?   12
THE SPECIAL CHARACTERISTICS OF AIKIDO   15

CHAPTER 2   ACQUIRING SKILL IN THE FUNDAMENTALS   21

KAMAE
1. DURING TRAINING YOU AND YOUR PARTNER MUST ASSUME A CORRECT *HANMI* STANCE   22
2. WHEN FACING A PARTNER, EITHER AN *AI-HANMI* OR *GYAKU-HANMI* STANCE CAN BE ASSUMED   24

UKEMI
1. BREAKFALLS TO THE BACK   26
2. FULL BACK BREAKFALL   30
3. BREAKFALLS TO THE FRONT   32
4. BREAKFALLS IN ACTUAL TRAINING   34
5. BREAKFALLS FOR PINNING TECHNIQUES   36

SHIKKO
MAINTAIN HANMI AND KEEP YOUR UPPER AND LOWER BODY AS ONE WHEN YOU MOVE   38

TE-GATANA
USE YOUR HAND-SWORDS TO PROJECT BREATH POWER   40

BODY MOVEMENT
1. *IRIMI*   44
2. *TENKAN* (turning)   48
3. *TENSHIN* (sweeping turn)   48

KOKYU-HO
1. *TACHI-WAZA KOKYU-HO (MOROTE-DORI KOKYU-HO OMOTE)*   50
2. *TACHI-WAZA KOKYU-HO (MOROTE-DORI KOKYU-HO URA)*   52
3. *SUWARI-WAZA KYOKU-HO*   54

**CHAPTER 3   TRAINING IN TECHNIQUES
—Acquisition of the Basics**   57

WHAT THINGS ARE INVOLVED IN AIKIDO TECHNIQUES?   58

NAGE-WAZA
1. *AI-HANMI-KATATE-DORI IRIMI-NAGE*   60
2. *SHOMEN-UCHI IRIMI-NAGE*   62
3. *KATATE-DORI SHIHO-NAGE (OMOTE)*   64

    4   *KATATE-DORI SHIHO-NAGE (URA)*   66

    5   *YOKOMEN-UCHI SHIHO-NAGE (OMOTE)*   68

    6   *YOKOMEN-UCHI SHIHO-NAGE (URA)*   70

    7   *RYOTE-DORI TENCHI-NAGE*   72

    8   *KATATE-DORI UCHI-KAITEN-NAGE*   74

    9   *KATATE-DORI SOTO-KAITEN-NAGE*   76

KATAME-WAZA

    1   *AI-HANMI KATATE-DORI DAI-IKKYO (OMOTE)*   78

    2   *AI-HANMI KATATE-DORI DAI-IKKYO (URA)*   80

    3   *SHOMEN-UCHI DAI-IKKYO (OMOTE)*   82

    4   *SHOMEN-UCHI DAI-IKKYO (URA)*   84

    5   *SHOMEN-UCHI DAI-IKKYO SUWARI-WAZA (OMOTE)*   86

    6   *SHOMEN-UCHI DAI-IKKYO SUWARI-WAZA (URA)*   88

    7   *GYAKU-HANMI KATATE-DORI DAI-IKKYO (OMOTE)*   90

    8   *GYAKU-HANMI KATATE-DORI DAI-IKKYO (URA)*   92

    9   *SHOMEN-UCHI DAI-NIKYO (OMOTE)*   94

  10   *SHOMEN-UCHI DAI-NIKYO (URA)*   98

  11   *KATA-DORI DAI-NIKYO (OMOTE)*   100

  12   *KATA-DORI DAI-NIKYO (URA)*   102

  13   *SHOMEN-UCHI DAI-SANKYO*   104

  14   *SHOMEN-UCHI DAI-SANKYO (URA)*   108

  15   *SHOMEN-UCHI DAI-YONKYO (OMOTE)*   110

  16   *SHOMEN-UCHI DAI-YONKYO (URA)*   112

NAGE-KATAME-WAZA

    1   *SHOMEN-UCHI KOTE-GAESHI*   114

    2   *KATATE-DORI KOTE-GAESHI*   116

    3   *TSUKI KOTE-GAESHI*   118

CHAPTER 4 ACQUIRING SKILL IN BASIC VARIATIONS   121

NAGE-WAZA

    1   *YOKOMEN-UCHI IRIMI-NAGE*   122

    2   *HANMI-HANTACHI KATATE-DORI SHIHO-NAGE*   124

    3   *HANMI-HANTACHI RYOTE-DORI SHIHO-NAGE (OMOTE)*   126

    4   *HANMI-HANTACHI RYOTE-DORI SHIHO-NAGE (URA)*   128

    5   *SHOMEN-UCHI KAITEN-NAGE*   130

KATAME-WAZA

    1   *YOKOMEN-UCHI DAI-IKKYO (OMOTE)*   132

    2   *YOKOMEN-UCHI DAI-IKKYO (URA)*   134

    3   *MOROTE-DORI DAI-NIKYO (OMOTE)*   136

    4   *MOROTE-DORI DAI-NIKYO (URA)*   138

    5   *USHIRO RYOTEKUBI-DORI DAI-SANKYO (OMOTE)*   140

    6   *USHIRO RYOTEKUBI-DORI DAI-SANKYO (URA)*   142

    7 YOKOMEN-UCHI DAI-YONKYO (OMOTE)   144
    8 YOKOMEN-UCHI DAI-YONKYO (URA)   146

CHAPTER 5 ACQUIRING SKILL IN APPLIED TECHNIQUE
—Advanced Training Methods   149

NAGE-WAZA
    1 MOROTE-DORI KOKYU-NAGE 1   150
    2 MOROTE-DORI KOKYU-NAGE 2   152
    3 MOROTE-DORI JUJI-GARAMI   154
    4 USHIRO RYOTEKUBI-DORI KOKYU-NAGE   156
    5 KATA-DORI SHOMEN-UCHI SHIHO-NAGE   158

KATAME-WAZA
    1 KATA-DORI SHOMEN-UCHI DAI-NIKYO (OMOTE)   160
    2 KATA-DORI SHOMEN-UCHI DAI-NIKYO (URA)   162
    3 USHIRO RYOKATA-DORI DAI-SANKYO (OMOTE)   164
    4 USHIRO RYOKATA-DORI DAI-SANKYO (URA)   166

NAGE-KATAME-WAZA
    1 MOROTE-DORI KOTE-GAESHI   168
    2 USHIRO RYOTEKUBI-DORI KOTE-GAESHI   170

TANTO-DORI
    1 TANTO-DORI YOKOMEN-UCHI DAI-GOKYO (OMOTE)   172
    2 TANTO-DORI YOKOMEN-UCHI DAI-GOKYO (URA)   176
    3 TANTO-DORI TSUKI-HIJI-GIME   178
    4 TANTO-DORI TSUKI-KOTE-GAESHI   180

FURTARI-DORI
    1 FUTARI-DORI 1   182
    2 FUTARI-DORI 2   184

CHAPTER 6 AIKIDO TRAINING PROCEDURES   187

REI-HO
    1 *REI* (Bowing with Respect)   188
    2 FORMALLY STANDING AND SITTING   189

WRIST WARM-UP EXERCISES
    KOTE-MAWASHI WARM-UP   190
    KOTE-GAESHI WARM-UP   191

SHIHO-NAGE BACK STRETCH EXERCISE   192

AFTER TRAINING STRETCH   194

TRAINING ATTIRE   195

CHAPTER 1

Introduction to Aikido Principles

WHAT IS AIKIDO?

Aikido as a Martial Art

Aikido is a system derived from the martial traditions of Japan. Martial arts that have preserved their traditions intact, as handed down from the past, are known as *kobudo*. Aikido, however, is not one of those *kobudo*. The founder of Aikido, Morihei Ueshiba, trained in many traditional martial art systems, and then developed Aikido, an entirely new system. Morihei took the best aspects of the old systems and created a martial art for the future, a modern Budo within the context of contemporary society.

There are other modern martial arts such as Judo, Kendo, and Karate-do, but these are all based on competition with sporting elements. Aikido, however, is free from organized competition, placing prime importance on individual spiritual development and social responsibility. Perhaps the most outstanding characteristic of Aikido is that it preserves the best aspects of the past within the framework of present social conditions to make it a pure, modern, universal Budo.

Aikido as a Training Method

Since Aikido does not have organized competitions, forging of the individual spirit is paramount. The Founder Morihei Ueshiba said, "Never cease forging your mind and body to refine your character though training—this is the first principle." In Aikido, we forge our body and mind, develop an unbreakable spirit, seek out the best in the human spirit, and train continually. This is the power of spiritual development.

The purpose of Aikido training is to harmonize oneself with nature, integrate body and mind, manifest one's inner goodness, activate one's spiritual power, and rest in a secure, unshakable state of being.

Aikido as Self-defense

Aikido is Budo, not a system of self-defense per se, and lacks any kind of organized competition. Human beings continually face dangers, however, and disasters can occur without warning. Aikido cannot protect us from unexpected dangers, but it does help us to develop presence of mind, and teaches us how to move in the most efficient manner, which can work as self-defense against unforeseen attacks. In the case of female practitioners, in training they learn how to control a stronger force and move quickly and properly; skills that can be applied in a practical and effective manner if the need should ever arise.

However, being able physically to overpower an attacker is not self-defense. Again, presence of mind is far more important, and avoiding dangerous situations first is the key to self defense, especially in the case of women. Stable presence of mind is what we develop daily in Aikido training.

Furthermore, in the modern world, we face a variety of dangers. Traffic, falling debris, earthquakes, fires, and the like are also our enemies. Aikido helps develop presence of mind—self-defense—against these threats as well.

Aikido for Mental Health

All those who practice Aikido notice, sooner or later, that because the movements of Aikido are based on natural principles, the balance between body and mind is naturally restored. In training, stress seems to disappear. Imperfections in one's character get ironed out. One develops a brighter outlook, a more positive attitude. In other words, a character that is "flexible on the outside, hard as diamond on the inside." We often see people who behave aggressively or are ruled by their passions, but among Aikido practitioners such people are rare. Aikido practitioners tend to be cheerful, not depressing, characters. They are not timid. In Aikido techniques, we learn how to project the power of *ki* in body and mind, and that helps dispel all inner stagnation.

Aikido for Physical Health

In Aikido, all the movements practiced are based on natural patterns. It is a balanced training method, and thus naturally good for the health. In modern daily life, total use of the body has been largely lost because of the reliance on machines, and this has a direct bearing on our health. In Aikido, there are many full body movements; movements that naturally stretch the outer and inner muscles and joints, and help keep us flexible. Aikido training also stimulates the nervous system, promoting good blood circulation. From the perspective of preventive medicine, this is this best kind of exercise.

Aikido as Life-long Education

Recently, it is not unusual to see children and parents training together in Aikido. Aikido is good for everyone regardless of age, and it is a valuable form of life-long education. Children, college students, adults—all ages benefit from developing the character and integration of the body and mind. Children who start the martial art of Aikido naturally settle down and learn good manners. In fundamental Aikido movements one learns how to project *ki*, and natural power—project it outward, not store it up inside. There is nothing forced in the natural movements of Aikido. Such training has a positive effect on one's character, making it brighter and more direct. The physical techniques of Aikido polish one's mind and body.

Aikido is popular among young people. It is traditional Budo, but free of sporting elements, and that makes it attractive to many active young people who wish to develop their entire persona—*ki*, mind, body, and power—as one. Aikido also helps relieve some of the pressure and strain young people experience.

For adults, the emphasis is more on maintaining the harmony of body and mind, good health, and spiritual refinement. In Aikido, we always try to keep ourselves focused in our *seika-tanden* (the body's psycho-physical center about two inches below the navel), and move with *ki*, body, and mind unified. With such a firm center it is easy to move freely and flexibly. Those who are naturally flexible on the outside yet strongly determined on the inside are respected by society. In Aikido, we have many practitioners of more advanced years. Since Aikido has many variations and the techniques can be adapted to meet one's physical needs, it helps keep your mind and body flexible. Even practitioners in their 80s can still conduct fulfilling and rewarding training in Aikido.

Aikido in the Context of Traditional Japanese Culture

After Japan's defeat in World War II, much of Japan's traditional culture was abandoned in the mad rush to develop into a world economic power. Nowadays, Japan is indeed an economic superpower, but upon reflection, much of our traditional spirit has been lost, and we are poorer for it. Today, many have forgotten the horrors of war, and the hard work that went into Japan's economic development. Now is the time to preserve the best elements of Japanese tradition.

In the past, Japanese people learned the values of venerable traditions, such as respect, trust, integrity, and determination. Aikido emerged from the ancient martial arts of Japan, not as a mere hobby or pastime, but as a true manifestation of Japanese traditional culture. Aikido is not a martial art that focuses on defeating an opponent; Aikido, many feel, is a Way leading to the perfection of the human character.

Aikido Fosters Relationships

As we have discussed, there are no forced movements in Aikido; everything is natural and harmonious. Aikido fosters good manners and integrity, and helps one develop a flexible yet firm character. Since Aikido enlightens those who honor peace, it is honored by the world at large.

From the beginning, Aikido never sanctioned organized competitions. It avoids all conflict, and emphasizes forging of body and mind. Within dedicated training, a spirit of harmony grows, and genuine friendship is found; and within friendship, there is unity. In Aikido, this is what creates lasting relationships.

Aikido is for everyone, in all parts of the globe. Aikido symbolizes harmony, love, and peace. Aikido is now practiced in nearly every country in the world, bringing people together—it is truly an international art.

THE SPECIAL CHARACTERISTICS OF AIKIDO

The Founder Morihei Ueshiba

What is *Ki*?

Aikido is a modern Budo established by Morihei Ueshiba, based on his intensive training in many different traditional Japanese martial art systems. As the name AI KI DO implies, it is centered on the principle of *ki*.

The term *ki* is utilized in various ways: in words such as *kuki* (air), *taiki* (atmosphere), and *joki* (steam), it represents phenomena that cannot be seen with the naked eye. We also have words like *satsuki* (bloodthirsty), *reiki* (spiritual), *seiki* (vitality), *kakki* (vigor), and *haki* (ambition) that describe active states that cannot be physically grasped. In Chinese thought as well, the theory of *ki* (*ch'i*) played a central role—Enami taught: "*Ki* is the fullness of existence." Going even further back, in ancient Indian philosophy, *ki* was called *prana*, the basic life stuff of the universe that also animates our individual existence.

In short, *ki* is the vital life-force that permeates existence, and it is the source of all energy.

Ki, Mind, and Body as One

The Founder Morihei Ueshiba, who researched the concept of *aiki* (harmonization of *ki*) deeply, explained *ki* like this: "*Ki* is the vital energy of the universe, and the subtle functioning of *ki* enlivens the five senses. Employ that force, with unity of body and mind, and you can move freely as you will."

How can we employ the subtle functioning of *ki*? First of all, we need to learn how to use our breath power (*kokyu-ryoku*). In Aikido, *ki* is actualized through breath power. As mentioned previously, the Indian philosophical term *prana* means "breath." It was an understanding of that eternal truth—the nature of universal breath—that led to the enlightenment of the Founder Morihei.

The Founder realized that it was necessary to unify mind, body, and *ki*. From that individual integration, one had to link oneself to the universe as a whole, and manifest the tremendous power of the life force. Ultimately, that harmonization—between *ki*, mind, and body—will result in true enlightenment. This is the purpose of Aikido.

Avoid Conflict, Do Not Fight

With *ki*, mind, and body unified, the universe appears in its true form, and anything that acts contrary to natural principles is immediately discerned; in this world of ours, there is no way to win over universal truths. With that mindset, in harmony with the universe, there is no way to lose. This is an invincible state of being, attained by winning without fighting.

The principle of winning by not fighting frees Aikido from the constraints of contests or matches. Right from the outset, Aikido is not concerned with victory or defeat, or the glory or disappointment of competition. Aikido is not a sport, consisting of winners and losers; it is a Budo for forging one's body and mind, a pure path.

Universal Patterns of Movement

In Aikido training, the primary objective is to harmonize oneself with universal patterns of movement, and naturally that is what we focus on first. Aikido has two basic forms of movement: *irimi* (entering) and *sabaki* (turning). *Irimi* is to enter directly on a straight line, while maintaining the possibility of spiral movement, to the side of an attack. *Sabaki* is the principle of circularity—movements that turn around an attack.

It is believed that our galaxy came into existence billions of years ago with a "big bang." This gave birth to countless stars, endlessly revolving at tremendous speeds. Our sun is one of those stars. Our planet revolves around the sun. Indeed, the universe is continually revolving and spinning. Likewise in Aikido, we enter, spiral, and turn, emulating these universal patterns.

Techniques that Embrace Harmony

In Aikido movements, harmony is paramount. Therefore, according to natural principles, the movements flow without hindrance. From one single, well-defined movement, many other movements can be freely applied. Movements should flow freely and consecutively without stagnation. Practice free flowing natural movements, and the harmony between mind and body will be restored with an exhilarating sense of fulfillment.

Since Aikido is Budo, we must control opponents in an instant, firmly and securely, but the best way of doing that is to employ the force of attack to our advantage, using our movement to neutralize an aggressive act in a flexible manner. The more flexibility employed, the more effective the technique. Thus, in Aikido techniques, a pliant and flexible mind and body is essential.

In Aikido techniques, we avoid all direct confrontation with an attacking force, and that is the special characteristic of our art. From one good technique, unlimited variations are born. This is the reason practitioners are encouraged to have an open mind and a wide spectrum of experiences.

The Search for Human Perfection

Most people view Aikido as a method of spiritual perfection. True, the practice of Aikido helps relieve stress, and can serve as a kind of psychotherapy, but it is not enough to see Aikido as purely a spiritual path. The ideal in Aikido is to unify one's *ki*, mind, and body. First, one trains to link the body with the universal patterns of nature; then one learns how to link one's mind to the truths of the universe, and finally the practitioner learns to integrate body, mind, *ki*, and the universe as one.

In this manner, the physical and spiritual aspects of life are harmonized in Aikido. That is why in Aikido there are physical techniques that foster the body, and mental techniques that develop the mind. Aikido is a way to cultivate human beings, a path for seekers of the truth. Above all, we must practice in the training hall, practice in daily life—practice Aikido from morning to night.

Technical Fundamentals

In order to master the various techniques of Aikido, there are several fundamental techniques that demand full knowledge. Mastery of these fundamental techniques allows one to advance. The initial elements one has to learn are the Aikido stance and Aikido movement. Movement in Aikido has two aspects: *irimi* (entering) and *sabaki* (turning). Then there is proper *ma-ai* (combative distance) and the correct use of the *te-gatana* (hand-sword), which is very important for the projection of breath power in Aikido. Let's look more closely at each of these fundamental techniques.

Stance (*kamae*)

In Aikido we employ a *hanmi* (half-body) stance. If the left foot is placed forward, it is called a *hidari-hanmi* stance; if the right foot is forward, it is called a *migi-hanmi* stance. All movements in Aikido begin and end with a *hanmi* stance, and we always face a partner in *hanmi*.

Regardless of whether the stance is to the right or to the left, the center of balance is maintained between both feet, enabling one freely to move the hips and knees. In a *hanmi* stance, it is relatively easy to avoid a thrust delivered from the front, and move freely front, back, right, or left. Furthermore, with a good *hanmi* stance it is possible to avoid attacks coming at once from several directions. Shifts from defense to attack, and attack to defense, can also be freely employed.

Whenever we move, it is always with a sliding step. There are a number of movements in Aikido, but the movement is always done with a sliding step.

Never step in with a bended knee, but use your whole body to move. Attacker or defender, always move with, and maintain, the *hanmi* stance.

Irimi

Irimi and *sabaki* are the two pillars of Aikido. When your partner attacks with a direct strike from the front, slide to the side of the attacking force, and enter deeply to his "dead angle." This is *irimi*. Correct *irimi* will render the opponent's attack ineffective.

This entering to the side of an attack with a sliding step and placing oneself in the opponent's dead angle is called "one step *irimi*." Once this single movement is mastered, it can be employed effectively against all attacks, armed or unarmed. Against a good *irimi*, entering completely, the opponent is helpless. This is a special characteristic of Aikido techniques.

When entering to the opponent's dead angle, do not bend your hips. Keep the hips and the rest of your body centered, the mind calm, and move in flexibly with "one step *irimi*."

Sabaki

Usually in Aikido, we enter to avoid an attack and then employ body turns to bring the attack under control. Such turns are spherical and very powerful. It is important to maintain a stable center in these turns, bringing your partner into your own sphere. You will thus break his posture, and bring him down with no trouble. Since he is within your sphere of movement, there is no way for him to break you down.

These circular movements are based on universal patterns. On a cosmic level, our entire solar system revolves around our sun; microcosmically, parts of atoms revolve around a nucleus. All of these things—the sun, the earth, atomic particles—are physical entities that spin and turn in harmony. This is a universal pattern.

Aikido movements are no different, and we call this the principle of circular movement. Circular movement has one other important aspect. When we look at a spinning top, the center of the top appears to be still. The outside is rapidly turning but the center is stable. In Aikido, we call that calm center *sumikiri*.

Irimi appears to be a direct movement but is in fact spherical, leading to the turning *sabaki* movements. This is one of the secrets hidden in the principle of circularity.

Ma-ai

The physical distance between you and your partner is known as "*ma*," and the combative tension between you and your partner is called "*ma-ai*." A proper and vital *ma-ai* makes it easier for your partner to deliver an attack, and for you to defend (and vice-versa). It is not simply a matter of assuming a certain distance. The various relationships between you and your partner—position, distance, direction [up, down, right, and left]—must be taken into account. The *ma-ai* and the technique applied in Aikido also subtly depends on how the partner is armed—with the hands, a knife, sword, staff, or long stick, etc. If one has a good *me-tsuke* (focus), an attack can immediately be discerned. Human beings signal their intended movement with their eyes. Use *me-tsuke* to read your partner's intentions and assume the proper *ma-ai*.

Te-gatana (Hand-sword)

In Aikido, we place great emphasis on the development of the life force and the projection of breath power. Concentration of physical, mental, and spiritual power in the *seika-tanden* is called *kokyu-ryoku*, breath power, in Aikido. It creates unlimited energy. Breath power is manifest in many varied techniques in Aikido, and there is a special set of exercises for breath power training.

Breath power in Aikido is most effectively manifest through the hand-swords. Using the hand-swords effectively and dynamically in various techniques is essential in Aikido. The hand-sword is a simple weapon, but employed with breath power it is a very strong force. In Aikido, the hand-sword is used in many ways—to strike, thrust, turn, block, receive, twist, pull, control, among others. In Aikido, we say, "Make a circle with the hands, and flow like water." Employ the hand-swords to move flexibly, harmoniously, and naturally with agile, quick, and sharp movements.

Omote (Front) and *Ura* (Back) Techniques

Aikido techniques are based on natural movements, and nature rests on the principles of yin and yang—negative and positive poles. In Aikido, we call movements to the front *omote* techniques and movements to the back *ura* techniques. Pinning techniques and throwing techniques all have *omote* or *ura* movements.

Omote Techniques

These techniques are characterized by entering movements; that is to enter to the dead angle of the opponent to control him. The movements are actually spherical but with a strong element of direct entering.

Ura Techniques

Here, one spins in a large circular motion to control the opponent. One turns around a stable center, draws the opponent into one's own sphere, and breaks his posture to control him. It is based on the principle of circularity.

The drum used at the Founder's dojo at Iwama.

CHAPTER 2

Acquiring Skill in the Fundamentals

KAMAE 1
DURING TRAINING YOU AND YOUR PARTNER MUST ASSUME A CORRECT *HANMI* STANCE

Keep your feet straight with your body centered between the front and back feet.

In the Aikido stance *ki*, mind, and body must be unified. Always face your partner in a *hanmi* stance. When the left foot is forward, the stance is *hidari-hanmi*; when the right foot is forward, the stance is *migi-hanmi*. The feet should be spaced about the width of one's shoulders; if the feet are too far apart, it is difficult to move quickly.

SHOMEN

Do not focus on any one point; set your gaze on your partner's entire body.

Face, abdomen, hips, and toes should be in a straight line when you face your partner.

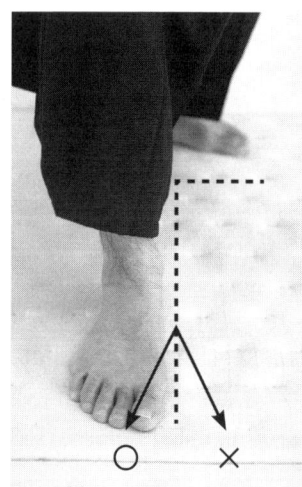

The feet form a rough right angle.

The front foot should be straight, or slightly open to the outside. It should never angle to the inside.

POINT: When Aikido techniques are practiced, the hanmi stance is important for both partners, from start to finish. A throwing technique, for example, almost always ends in hanmi.

SIDE VIEW

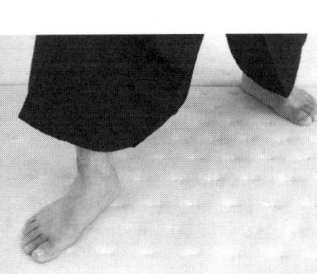

The hips should be centered between the legs.

The knees should be relaxed and flexible.

KAMAE 2

WHEN FACING A PARTNER, EITHER AN *AI-HANMI* OR *GYAKU-HANMI* STANCE CAN BE ASSUMED

Hanmi is the basis of all movement.

Both *ai-hanmi* or *gyaku-hanmi* stances can be assumed when facing an opponent. When both partners have the opposite foot forward, it is *gyaku-hanmi*; when they both have the same foot forward, it is *ai-hanmi*. The *hanmi* stance facilitates attacking and defending, changing direction, or dealing with multiple attacks. Assuming a correct stance is the first step in Aikido training.

GYAKU-HANMI

Here, tori has his right foot forward; uke has his left foot forward. This is called *migi-gyaku-hanmi*. If *tori* had his left foot forward, and *uke* his right foot, it would be called *hidari-gyaku-hanmi*.

Tori has his right foot forward in a *hanmi* stance; *uke* has his left foot forward. This is a *migi-gyaku-hanmi* stance.

Both partners are well centered and facing each other directly. Such a good mutual stance allows for proper execution of the techniques; however, if you and your partner are not synchronized you cannot practice correctly.

AI-HANMI

Both partners have the same foot forward in *hanmi*. In this case, it is the right foot, so it is called *migi-ai-hamni*. The reverse stance, with the left feet forward, is *hidari-ai-hanmi*.

Both *tori* and *uke* have the right foot forward. This is a *migi-ai-hanmi* stance.

TERMINOLOGY

Tori is the partner who applies the technique; *uke* is the one who receives the technique. In this book, execution of the techniques from only one side is shown, but in actual training, techniques are always practiced from both sides.

UKEMI 1
BREAKFALLS TO THE BACK
In all breakfalls, keep the chin in, and role circularly

1

Side View

2

Bend your toes, don't stand on them.

Set one knee firmly before rolling.

3: Drop one knee to the mat.

6–8: Roll back up quickly. Be ready to move as soon as you are back on your feet.

From the knees, roll with your thighs, hips, and back touching the mat in that order.

Keep your chin pulled in, far enough to be able to see the knot on your belt.

4–5: After the knees, follow with the thighs, hips, and back.

From your knees to your back, roll in the proper order.

Breakfalls, *ukemi*, are for the protection of the body when thrown or knocked down. Always fall lightly and circularly in the direction of the throw or pin, following that force, but then spring back up, ready to move. The basic back breakfall is illustrated here.

UKEMI 1
BREAKFALLS TO THE BACK

Back breakfall in rear view

1–2: Bend your back leg to initiate the breakfall.

3: Set your back knee to the mat.

6–7: Use a rocking motion to spring right up, ready to move.

4–5: Bring your thighs, hips, and back down to the mat; keep the chin firmly pulled in when hitting the mat.

POINT: In movements 1–4, bring your body down in the proper order. If thrown down quickly, the head may hit the ground, and this is very dangerous.

UKEMI 2

FULL BACK BREAKFALL
The left knee over the right shoulder with a full rollover

Side View

1–2: Use the front knee to lower the body.

3: After the knee, bring the thighs and hips down.

4: The back and shoulder touch the mat. Then roll over with the left hip, back, and right shoulder.

Don't throw yourself down suddenly, use the knee to sink to the mat. This breakfall is very dangerous for beginners, so learn it slowly and correctly.

Use the front knee to bring yourself down, and roll over close to the ground.

This is a full turn back breakfall. Points to note:
(1) Use the knees to lower yourself to the mat, and roll over close to the ground.
(2) Do not roll straight back, use your arms and shoulders to roll over diagonally. (3) Roll in a circle, with all parts of the body touching the mat smoothly.

POINT: Roll over diagonally with the left arm and right shoulder. If you roll straight backward over your head, it is easy to injure the neck.

Rear View

1 **2** **3**

5–7: After the full turn, spring up, and be ready to move.

4　　　　　5　　　　　6　　　　　7

UKEMI 3

BREAKFALLS TO THE FRONT
Toes to the front, and roll over

Side View

1: Bend the front knee slightly, and lower the body.

2: Bend both knees, and extend the front hand downward.

3: Place the front arm in the direction in which you want to roll.

POINT: Place the front hand in the direction you want to roll, with the fingers lightly spread. Keep the arm nicely curved—it should be an aid, not a hindrance, to rolling.

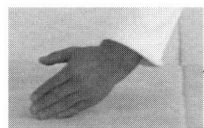

Roll over in a slightly diagonal position.

Roll forward smoothly and spring right up ready to move.

If you do not extend your hands and fingers in the direction you want to roll, they act as a brake, and you cannot roll well.

Roll diagonally over your shoulders and hip, and use the front knee to stand.

Roll over with the left shoulder, right hip, and right knee.

Front View

1 **2** **3**

4–5: Roll over on the back of the shoulder, then hips.    **6–7:** Roll completely up and be ready to move.

> It is not necessary for beginners to learn this from a standing position. They may start the roll from a seated position.

4   **5**   **6**   **7**

UKEMI 4
BREAKFALLS IN ACTUAL TRAINING
Using the breakfalls you have practiced in real situations

The back breakfall for *katate-dori shiho-nage*

1–2: When *uke* grasps *tori*'s right wrist, *tori* enters to *uke*'s side.   **3–4:** *Tori* raises his hand-swords and turns.

The back breakfall of *irimi-nage*

Uke moves in *hanmi*, following *tori*'s lead.

Do not push down too far on *uke*'s neck, or step too far in.

1–2: As soon as *uke* raises his hand-sword, *tori* uses his hand-sword to control him, enters to his side, and holds his neck.   **3:** *Tori* turns while cutting down on *uke*'s arm and guides him around.

Front breakfall for *katate-dori kokyu-nage*

In photographs 2 and 3, *uke* follows *tori*'s movement while holding his wrist tightly; if *uke* lets go, the technique will stop. *Uke* must blend with the movement of *tori*'s hand-sword and push off the rear foot to avoid injury.

1–2: As soon as *uke* grabs *tori*'s front wrist, *tori* enters to *uke*'s side.

Breakfalls with a partner are basically the same as those done on your own.

The breakfalls we introduced on the previous pages were all done individually, but here we will demonstrate how to execute them with a partner. In actual practice: follow through to the end, don't stop your movement, making it difficult for your partner to apply the technique. In rear breakfalls, roll over naturally and smoothly with the knees, thighs, hips, and back; in front breakfalls, use the hands, arms, and shoulders to roll over properly.

Uke should follow *tori*'s movement, not moving too quickly or too slowly.

Uke falls to the same side as the hand used to grab *tori*'s wrist.

In this technique, *tori* keeps a tight grip on *uke*'s arm; if he lets go, *uke* may get injured.

5–6: *Tori* cuts down on *uke*'s wrist and throws him.

Uke should spin on his feet, and not lose contact with *tori*.

Uke should take a natural back breakfall, with the knees, thighs, hips, and back touching the ground in that order.

4: *Tori* raises his arm.   **5–7:** *Tori* steps in and cuts down with his arm, effecting the throw.

Uke must hold tightly to *tori*'s wrist to the very end.

3–6: While turning, *tori* cuts down with his hand-sword to throw *uke* to the front.

Uke must roll over naturally with hand, arm, shoulder, back, and hips lightly touching the mat.

UKEMI 5
BREAKFALLS FOR PINNING TECHNIQUES
Use your knees to take a good breakfall.

The breakfall for pinning techniques (*omote*)

1

> *Tori* controls *uke*'s elbow and shoulder flexibly; *uke* should not resist unduly.

2–3: *Tori* controls the attacking arm with his hand-sword, grasps *uke*'s elbow, and enters to the front.

> In pinning techniques, it is essential not to tighten up or resist the techniques. If you are stiff, you can get hurt. Keep the body flexible and relaxed, and take the breakfall with your entire body.

> *Uke* should remain centered while blending with *tori*'s movements.

The breakfall for pinning techniques (*ura*)

1

2: *Uke* keeps his upper body relaxed, *tori* controls his arm with his hand-sword and a grip on his elbow.

3–4: While turning, *tori* cuts down on *uke*'s arm.

> Keep the knees flexible. Do not bend your hips; follow the turning movement, blend with it, and sink to the ground naturally.

Use your front hand to break the fall, and do not tighten up.

In pinning techniques, *uke* ends up face down on the mat. The key here is to lower yourself down with the hands and knees. On the mat, do not tighten up or try to avoid the pin; follow *tori*'s pinning movements.

4–5: *Tori* cuts down on *uke*'s arm and moves forward.

6: *Tori* pins *uke* to the mat.

Uke uses his front hand to ease himself to the mat.

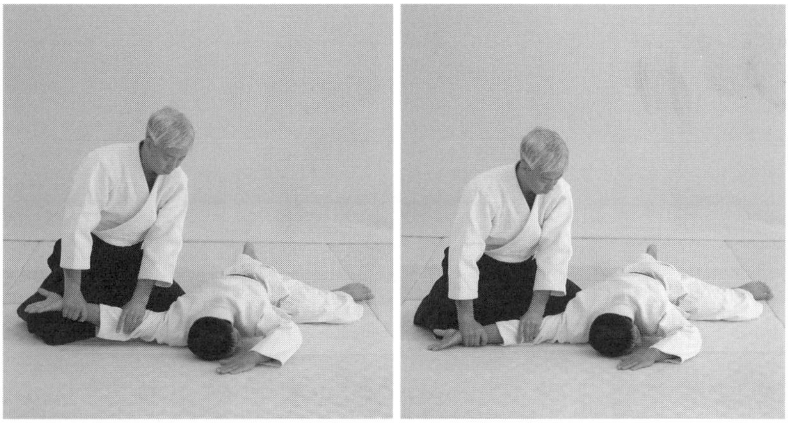

5–6: *Uke* is pinned face down on the mat.

As in photographs 3–4, *uke* should keep his center of gravity low, and move his knees then hands (vice-versa is also fine) to the ground.

SHIKKO
MAINTAIN HANMI AND KEEP YOUR UPPER AND LOWER BODY AS ONE WHEN YOU MOVE

Move forward on the knees while turning the hips. Keep the feet together, always walk on your toes.

POINT: The angle of the knees should be within 90 degrees.

1: From a seated position

2: Stand on your toes.

3: Walk on your toes, moving right and left.

7: Pivot on the knees.

8: Keeping your center of gravity low, move forward.

9: Stand on your toes, feet together.

Turn with your hips and move forward on your knees.

Shikko, "knee walking," is used in the many seated techniques of Aikido, and is one of its most important aspects. Knee walk on your toes, moving forward or backward, or making turns, without breaking your posture. Keep a good balance between the hips and knees, keep your hands and upper body straight, and maintain a proper posture throughout.

POINT: Keep your center of gravity low as you move, making it easy to move from side to side, and to turn smoothly.

Point: (See the explanation below)

If the upper body is too far forward when you move, it will weaken your hip turns.

4: Keep your center of gravity low as you move on your knees.

5: Turn your hips in using the front knee as a pivot.

6: Keep your center of gravity low.

10: Return to the *seiza* position.

POINT: As illustrated in photos 3–5, keep the upper and lower body together as you move from side to side on your knees. Don't move your arms or turn the body because this will cause you to lose your balance.

39

TE-GATANA
USE YOUR HAND-SWORDS TO PROJECT BREATH POWER

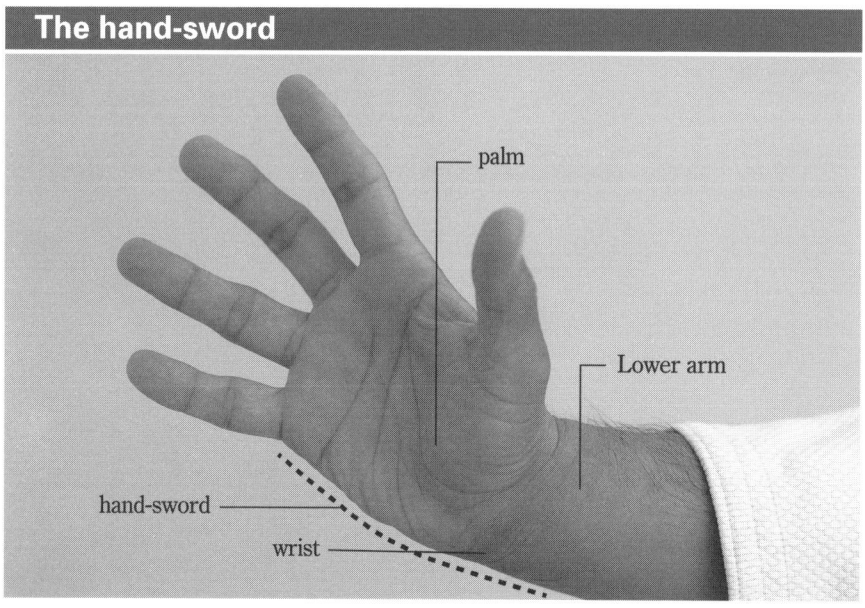

The hand-sword

- palm
- Lower arm
- hand-sword
- wrist

The hand-sword consists of not just the hand; the palm, wrist, and lower arm are involved. Also, power is generated with the entire body through the hand-swords, not just with the arm.

The different aspects of a hand-sword

Employ the hand-sword as a weapon to block, to receive, and so on—in Aikido we use breath power to control an opponent, and project that power through the hand-swords. The hand-sword can be employed many ways: to strike, to thrust, to turn, to block, to receive, to twist, to pull, to hold, etc. In the techniques, we use these hand-sword movements to break *uke*'s posture and control him. Here are some of the ways a hand-sword is employed:

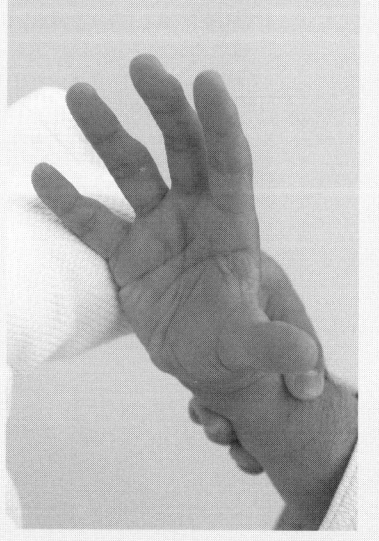

Extending upward (e.g.-*ten-chi-nage*)

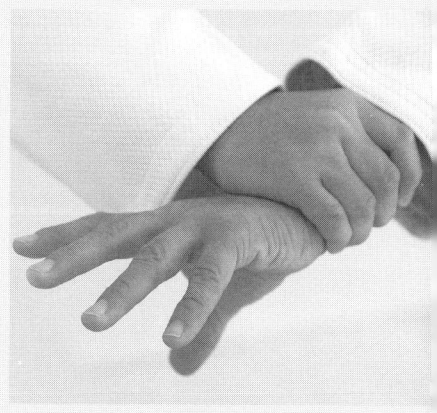

Sweeping to the side (e.g.-*uchi-kaiten-nage, ten-chi-nage*)

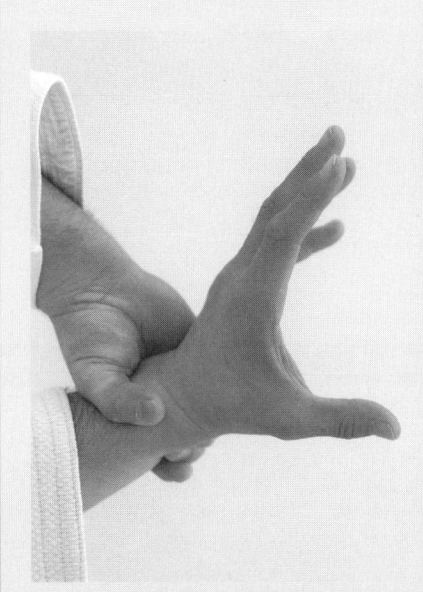

From the inside (e.g.-*uchi-kaiten-nage*) 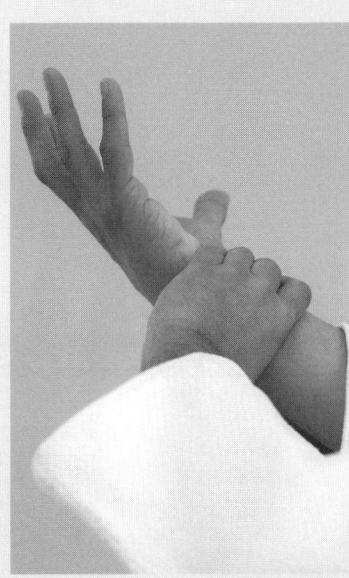 Cutting down (e.g.-*kokyu-ho*) 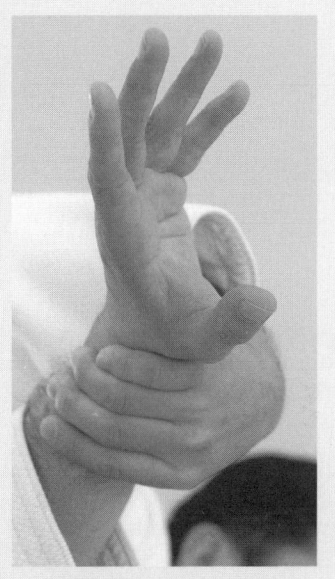 From the side (e.g.-*soto-kaiten-nage*)

Controlling a *yokomen-uchi* attack (e.g.-*yokomen-uchi dai-ikkyo ura*, see pp. 134–135)

TE-GATANA

Using the hand-sword in body turns

1: *Uke* grasps *tori*'s wrist in this manner.

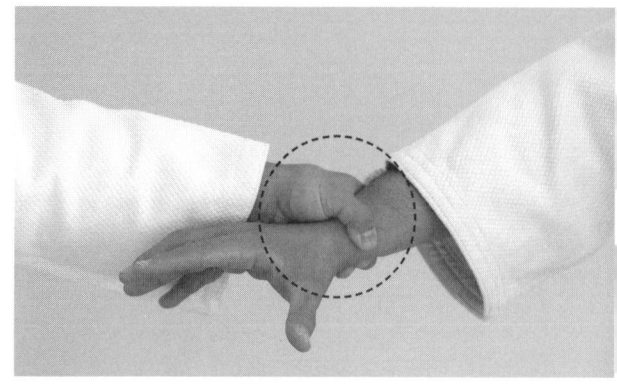

2: Do not pull or push this section.

Using the hand-sword to break your partner's grip 1

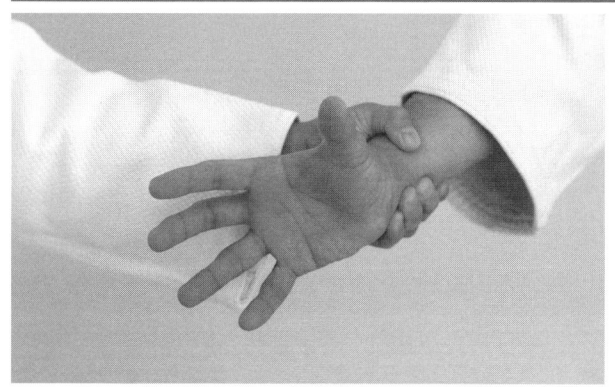

1: *Uke* grabs *tori*'s wrist in this manner.

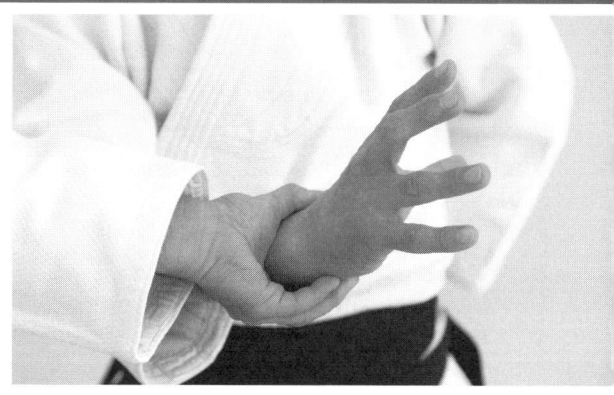

2: Keeping your arm close to the body, turn your elbow in and begin to release his grip.

Using the hand-sword to break your partner's grip 2

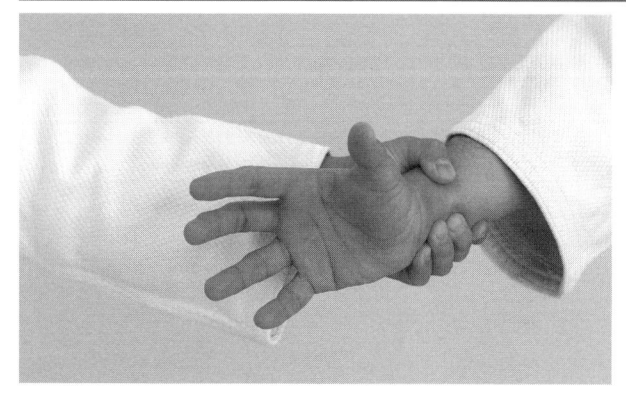

1: *Uke* grabs *tori*'s wrist in this manner.

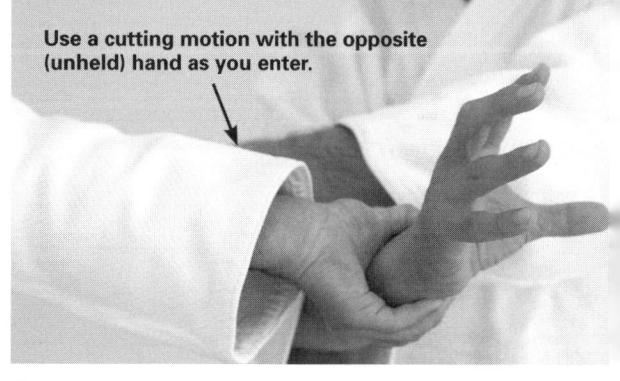

Use a cutting motion with the opposite (unheld) hand as you enter.

2: Slip your opposite arm under his arm with a cutting motion as you enter.

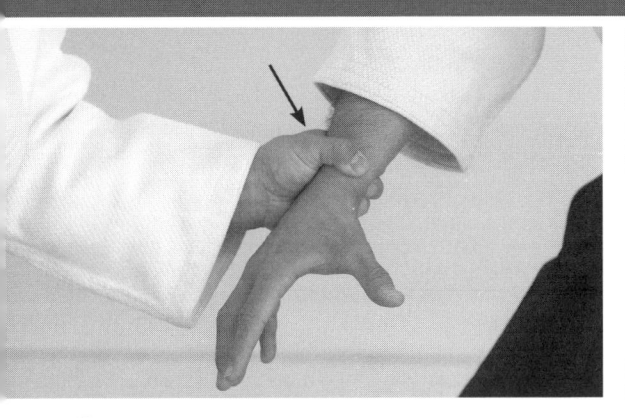

3: Enter and turn while maintaining your center of gravity.

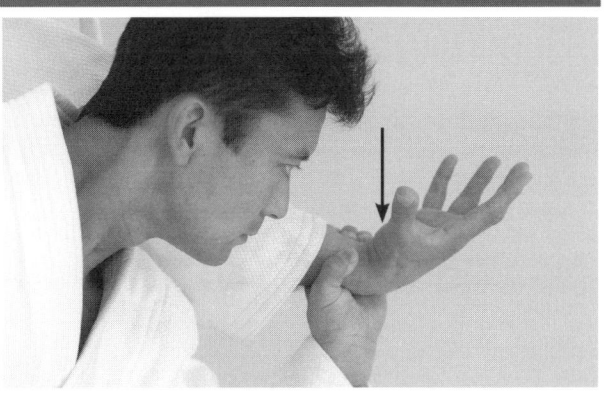

4: While entering and turning, use your hand-sword to break *uke*'s posture.

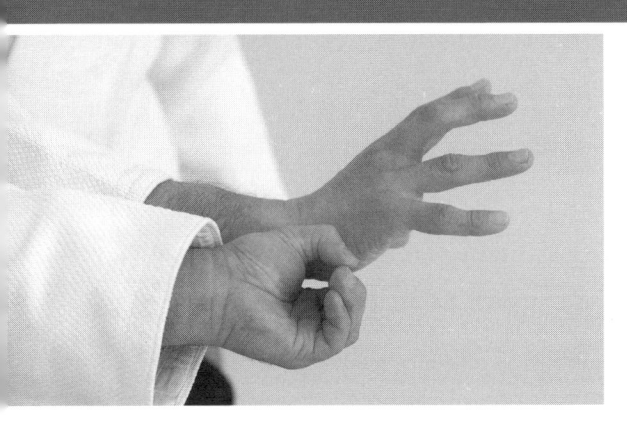

3: Turn your hand-sword in the space between his four fingers and his thumb, and release the grip.

3: Release his grip by turning your hand-sword in the space between his four fingers and thumb, and pressing out with your opposite hand. After the release keep the opposite hand on his arm.

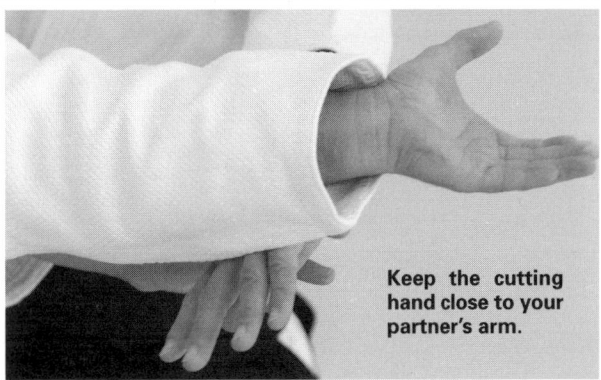

4: Keep the opposite hand on your partner's arm. Use both hand-swords in this technique.

Keep the cutting hand close to your partner's arm.

43

BODY MOVEMENT 1 *IRIMI*
Harmonize entering movements and the use of the hand-swords

Entering to the Side 1

1: The partners are in the *migi-gyaku-hanmi* stance.

2: *Uke* steps in and grasps *tori*'s wrist.

Entering to the Side 2

1: In the *migi-ai-hanmi* stance.

2: *Uke* steps in and grabs *tori*'s wrist.

In Aikido, both fundamental and advanced techniques employ the same basic body movements. The essential movements do not change. The basic movements in Aikido are *irimi* (entering), *tenkan* (turning), and *tenshin* (sweeping turns). If these movements are mastered, they can be applied in many varied techniques.

The entering movement.

3–4: *Tori* steps in with the back foot as he enters raising his hand-sword. He keeps his body centered between the feet as he moves.

5: *Tori* cuts down with his hand-sword and extends *uke*'s body fully.

The entering movement.

3: *Tori* steps in with the back foot to *uke*'s side and raises his hand-sword as shown on pp. 72–73.

4: *Tori* cuts down with his hand-sword, breaking *uke*'s posture, and extends his body fully.

45

BODY MOVEMENT 1 *IRIMI* (Continued)

Entering to the Side 3

1: In the *hidari-gyaku-hanmi* stance.

2: *Uke* steps to grab *tori*'s wrist; *tori* immediately enters with his front foot.

Entering to the Side and Turning Inside

1: In the *hidari-gyaku-hanmi* stance.

2: *Uke* steps in and grabs *tori*'s wrist.

Entering to the Side and Turning Outside

1: In the *hidari-gyaku-hanmi* stance.

2: *Uke* steps in and grabs *tori*'s wrist.

Atemi (preemptive strike)

Use the atemi to break uke's posture.

3: *Tori* delivers *atemi* while entering to *uke*'s side, sliding in with the back foot.

4: *Tori* keeps *uke*'s arm fully extended out. From this position, it should be easy to move in any direction.

3: *Tori* delivers *atemi* while entering to *uke*'s side, sweeps out with his hand-sword, and makes a full turn to the front.

4: After turning inside, *tori* is in the *hanmi* stance, as illustrated here.

3: *Tori* enters to the outside while raising his hand-sword, and turns to the outside.

4: After turning to the outside, *tori* is in the *hanmi* stance.

BODY MOVEMENT 2 *TENKAN* (turning)

Use the front foot as a pivot when you turn.

Using the front foot as a pivot in turns is called *tenkan.* Turning in harmony with the movement of the hand-swords, it is possible to break your partner's posture. Keep the knees flexible, the body stable, turn in big circles, and guide your partner into your own sphere.

1: In *migi-gyaku-hanmi*.

2–3: *Uke* steps in and grabs *tori*'s wrist.

BODY MOVEMENT 3 *TENSHIN* (sweeping turn)

While keeping your body stable, turn circularly, and guide your partner.

The body movement here is basically the same as *tenkan,* but with more of a sweep to control your partner. In the technique shown here, *tori* uses the force of the attacking *yokomen* strike to his advantage.

1: In the *hidari-ai-hanmi* stance.

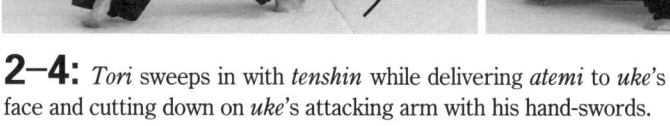

2–4: *Tori* sweeps in with *tenshin* while delivering *atemi* to *uke*'s face and cutting down on *uke*'s attacking arm with his hand-swords.

Taking care not to clash with the flow of your partner's power, turn.

4: While turning his hand-sword upward, *tori* enters and turns in the direction indicated.

5: After the turn, *tori* finishes in a well-balanced stance. *Tori* must use *uke*'s power when he turns, and not lose his own center of gravity.

When *uke* strikes, immediately respond by stepping in, cutting down with the hand-swords, and employ the attacking force to your advantage with the *tenshin* movement.

Tori sweeps around with the back foot while blending with *uke*'s strike.

5: After completing the *tenshin* turn, *tori* can lead *uke* in any direction he likes.

KOKYU-HO 1
MANIFEST THE POWER OF YOUR ENTIRE BODY; MANIFEST BREATH POWER BY TRAINING IN BREATH DEVELOPMENT EXERCISES

Tachi-waza kokyu-ho (morote-dori kokyu-ho omote)

1: In the *gyaku-hanmi* stance.

2–3: From the side, *uke* cuts down on *tori*'s arm and grabs it with both hands.

Tori moves from his center as he enters to *uke*'s side.

4: *Tori* steps in with his back foot, remains centered, and enters while raising his hand-sword.

5–6: *Tori* steps behind *uke*, and cuts down with his hand-swords to break *uke*'s posture and bring him down. *Tori* keeps his gaze to the front, and his back foot firmly set on the ground.

As illustrated in photos 3–4, *tori* employs full use of his hips and feet as he raises his hand-sword.

Keep in mind that in *kyoku-ho* the purpose is not to throw your partner, but to develop your own breath power. Beginners need to develop the proper form, so it is important for partners to work together.

7: *Tori* throws *uke* and finishes with *zanshin* (alert posture).

In Aikido, one makes use of one's natural power, in a concentrated form, to down and control an opponent. The development of this power, and the proper use of the hand-swords, feet, and hips is called *kokyu-ryoku*, breath power, in Aikido. In order to foster such power, we have a series of exercises called *kokyu-ho*—breath exercises. There are many *kokyu* techniques in Aikido, but here we will introduce the most fundamental: standing and sitting *kokyu-ho*.

In the case of standing *kokyu-ho*, note the following:

When your partner grabs your arm, keep that as your focal point, and concentrate your power there. Doing this will ensure no power is wasted as you raise your hand-sword.

When your partner grabs your wrist, keep your hand-sword in the center of the movement. As you raise your arm, do not use just the strength in your arms; use your hips and feet as well. In fact, use your entire body to move in harmony.

Keep these points in mind as you train in *kokyu-ho*.

Good and bad examples of grabbing the arm

Uke grabs *tori*'s arm from the side. This is a good example.

○

Do not grab the arm from the front. This is a bad example.

✕

KOKYU-HO 2

POWER ALSO COMES FROM THE FEET AND HIPS WHEN THE HAND-SWORD IS RAISED

Tachi-waza kokyu-ho (morote-dori kokyu-ho ura)

1: In the *gyaku-hanmi* stance.

2–3: *Uke* cuts down on *tori*'s arm and grabs it with both hands.

> Keep your power focused in your hand-sword and use your entire body to move; if you just use the power in your arms, it will not be sufficient. Use the power of the turning movement as well.

7–8: *Tori* takes a large step behind *uke*, and cuts down with both hand-swords.

Keep yourself centered when you raise the hand-swords. In this case, *tori* turns when his arm is grabbed, but as in the previous example, he keeps centered as he raises his hand-sword, and throws *uke*. In *kokyu-ho*, you must use the power of your feet and hips as well as your arms. Train like this, and you can utilize the full power of your body.

4–6: *Tori* uses the front foot as a pivot, and with his body and hand-sword centered, makes a strong turn to break *uke*'s posture.

As illustrated in photos 4–6, stay centered when you enter and turn. This will result in the optimum projection of your power.

9–10: *Tori* throws *uke*, finishing in *zanshin*.

KOKYU-HO 3

USE YOUR HIPS AND ABDOMEN TO GENERATE POWER, AND RAISE YOUR PARTNER'S ARMS

Suwari-waza kyoku-ho

1: In the *seiza* position.

2: *Uke* grabs *tori*'s wrists from the side.

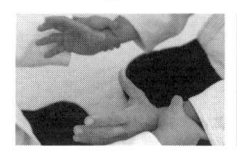

POINT 1: Grab your partner's wrists from the side; keep a tight grip throughout the exercise.

4–6: *Tori* steps forward on either foot and cuts down with both hand-swords.

Relax your hands, arms, and shoulders

Here you face your partner in *seiza*; you let him grab both of your wrists, and practice *kokyu-ho*. You do not push with your arms, but rather generate power from your hips to raise his arms, breaking his posture. In seated techniques such as this, be careful not to lean too far forward or too far back; concentrate your power in your lower abdomen. Do not try to put too much force in your hands, arms, or shoulders; use the power generated from your abdomen to control your partner.

Do not raise your shoulders.

Get your partner's arms up.

Do not rise up on your knees.

POINT 2: Do not push your partner. Use the power generated from your hips and abdomen concentrated in your hand-swords to raise your partner's arms. When his arms are raised against his sides like this, his power is lost, and it is easy to bring him down by cutting down. *Uke* must try to retain his grip to the end.

3

Do not push with the arms, generate your power from the abdomen like this.

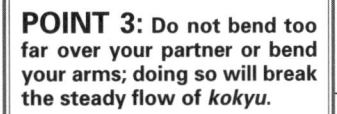

POINT 3: Do not bend too far over your partner or bend your arms; doing so will break the steady flow of *kokyu*.

Pin your partner's center. In training, be careful about the distance and placement of the pin; don't just try to hold him down with physical force.

7: *Tori* pins *uke* with both arms. *Tori* stands on his toes during the pin.

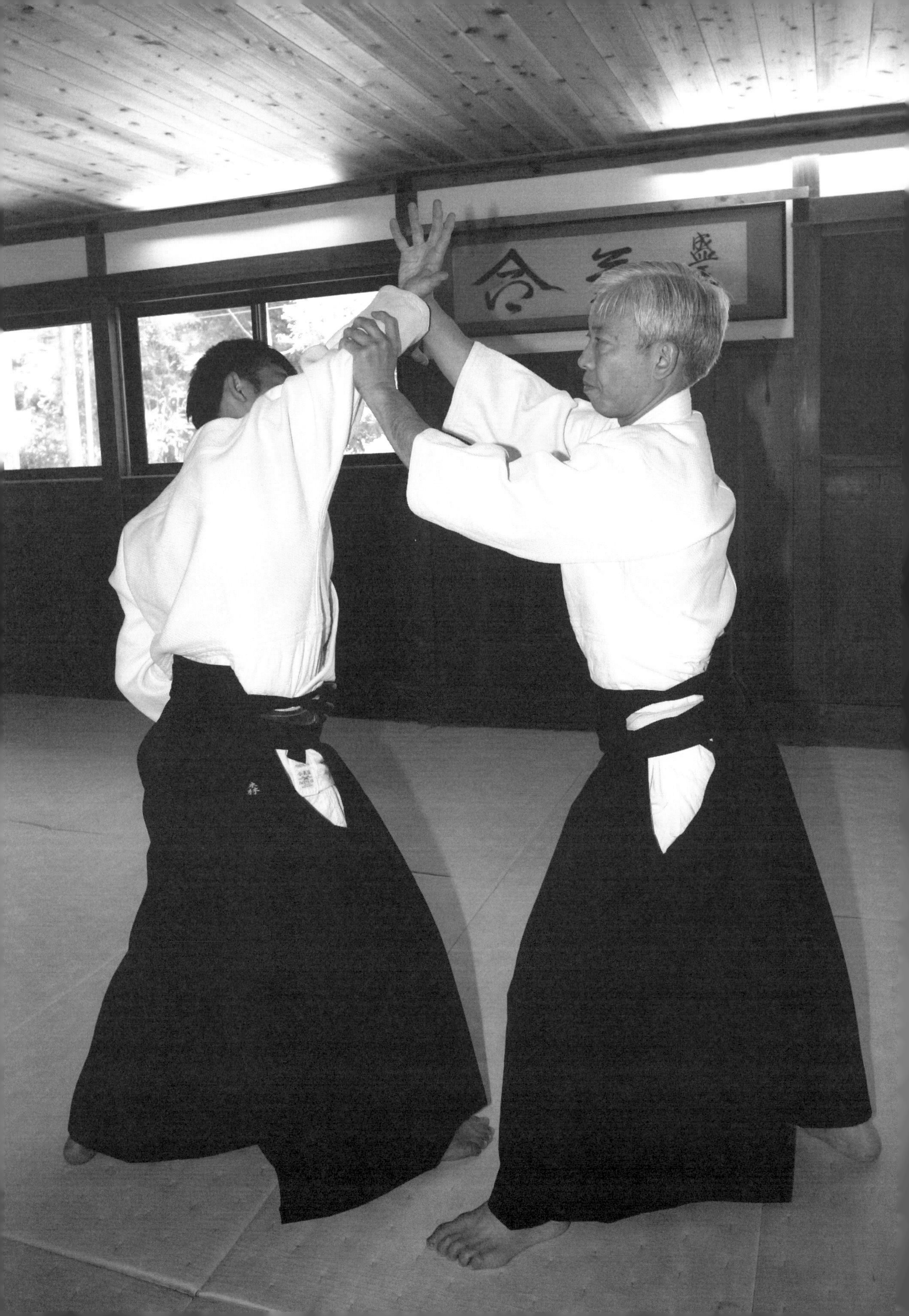

CHAPTER 3

Training in Techniques

Acquisition of the Basics

WHAT THINGS ARE INVOLVED IN AIKIDO TECHNIQUES?

Aikido has many techniques. Prior to actually practicing them, we need a basic understanding of the different elements in Aikido training. Aikido techniques are divided into two main pillars: *tanren-ho* (forging methods) and *gi-ho* (technical methods).

> 1. *Tanren-ho*: seated techniques, one partner seated one partner standing techniques, standing techniques, and techniques against weapons—four methods of forging in all.
>
> 2. *Gi-ho*: Pinning techniques, throwing techniques, and throw-and-pin techniques—three kinds of technical elements.

Actually, it is rather difficult to separate 1 and 2 distinctly, but for the sake of clarity, in this book we have grouped the techniques into throws, pins, and throws-and-pins.

1 TANREN-HO

***Suwari-waza* (seated techniques).** Here both partners are seated in *seiza*. Rising up on the toes, *tori* uses the hips and knees to move and control *uke*, all the while retaining good balance.

***Hanmi-hantachi-waza* (one partner seated, one standing techniques).** Here, *uke* stands while *tori* remains seated, and he deals with the attack with a pin or throw. *Tori* moves in *hanmi* even on the ground, entering and turning, and this strengthens the hips and lower body.

***Tachi-waza* (standing techniques).** Here, both partners are standing, and *tori* can freely use any technique he chooses against an attack by *uke*. This is the best way to train in *ma-ai*, use of the hand-swords, entering, and turning. There are many standing techniques, and most of the techniques introduced in this book are *tachi-waza*.

***Buki-waza* (techniques against armed attacks).** Here, *uke* is armed with a weapon such as a knife, sword, or staff. *Tori* can face him unarmed or armed. This type of technique is good for training in *ma-ai*, since the distance involved depends greatly on the length of the weapon.

2 GI-HO

***Katame-waza* (pinning techniques).** Here, *tori* controls *uke*'s attack with a good entry and powerful turns, applies locks to his joints, and then pins him face down. The locks are divided into four main groups: arm pins, twisting pins, turning pins, and pulse pins.

***Nage-waza* (throwing techniques).** These are the throwing techniques of Aikido: basic throws such as *irimi-nage*, *shiho-nage*, *kaiten-nage*, and more advanced throws such as *tenchi-nage*, *kokyu-nage*, *koshi-nage*, and *aiki-nage*.

***Nage-katame-waza* (throw-and-pin techniques).** After *uke* is thrown with the appropriate movements, he is then pinned to the ground by having his joints controlled.

NAGE-WAZA 1

AI-HANMI-KATATE-DORI IRIMI-NAGE
If your entry is too shallow it will be difficult to break your partner's posture

1

Point (see explanation below)

2–3: When *uke* grabs *tori*'s wrist, *tori* immediately raises his front hand-sword.

As illustrated in photos 5–7, make the sweeping turn and the cutting down of the hand-sword together.

Turn and cut down.

6–7: *Tori* uses his front foot as a pivot, and breaks *uke*'s posture.

Keep your partner's neck against your shoulder during the turn.

POINT: *Uke*'s movement within the entire technique.
Uke plays a critical role in Aikido, and a good *uke* always keeps in mind these points:
—Maintain *hanmi* when you move.
—Do not break contact with *tori*; always move and take breakfalls naturally.
—Follow *tori*'s lead, and do not lose the flow of the technique.

1: Hold tight to *tori*'s wrist, keep in contact.

2: Do not let go of *uke*'s neck.

Make the turn and the cutting down of the hand-sword together in one movement. When beginner students first attempt to apply *irimi-nage* they usually stiffen up. We use this technique to help break that habit, and help both partners develop a good flow. (The following technique *shomen-uchi irimi-nage* is also good for this.) *Tori* should enter deeply, keeping his body in contact with *uke*. *Uke* should remain relaxed and flexible, and not plant his feet on the ground.

How to enter

4–5: *Tori* enters deeply to *uke*'s side while controlling his neck.

> You must make a big sweeping move here. If your entry is too shallow, the *ma-ai* will be too close, and you will find it difficult to throw your partner.

8–10: *Tori* steps in deeply and cuts down with this hand-sword to throw *uke*.

3: *Uke* should keep his body relaxed, and not break contact with *tori*.

4: Keep the knees flexible.

5: Always follow *tori*'s lead, even when going down.

61

NAGE-WAZA 2

SHOMEN-UCHI IRIMI-NAGE
When you enter, keep your body in *hanmi*.

1: In the *ai-hanmi* stance.

Do not try to throw your partner with just your hands or feet. As illustrated in photos 3–6, cut down and move together, and use your entire body to break his posture.

Tori immediately blends to *uke*'s attack.

2: As soon as *uke* attacks, *tori* enters to his side.

3–6: *Tori* controls *uke*'s neck and hand-sword, pivots on the front foot, breaks his posture, and leads him.

7–9: *Tori* takes a big step in, cuts down with his hand-sword, and throws *uke*. *Tori* assumes *zanshin* after the throw.

Use your entire body to break your partner's posture.

In *irimi-nage*, *tori* avoids the attack by sliding to the side, and uses a powerful turn to break his partner's posture and throw him. Since there are many *irimi-nage* techniques in Aikido, it is necessary to have a good understanding of the basic technique:

—When *tori* enters he must remain in *hanmi*.
—*Tori* uses his grip on *uke*'s neck and his hand-sword to break *uke*'s posture.
—Make the turn and the cutting down of the hand-sword in unison, making use of the attacking force to lead and throw *uke*.

Use your shoulder to lead your partner.

POINT: When *tori* enters his body is in *hanmi*. *Tori* controls *uke*'s neck and hand-sword to break his posture.

After entering, *tori* has both feet parallel in *hanmi*. Make sure the hips are in, and the back straight.

Sweep with the back foot.

Control with the hand-sword.

NAGE-WAZA 3

KATATE-DORI SHIHO-NAGE (OMOTE)
Make full use of your hand-sword as you enter

Harmonize the movement of your hand-sword and the entering movement of your body.

In *shiho-nage*, you use the front foot as a pivot to turn and cut in four (or eight) directions and throw your partner. In this technique, the relationship between the movement of the hand-sword and the movement of the body in Aikido is at its clearest. It is one of the basic Aikido movements.

Training repeatedly in this technique imparts good understanding of hand-sword movement in Aikido, and teaches you how to turn naturally. The point we want to emphasize most here is that *tori* makes full use of his hand-sword as he enters. He turns his hand inside as he enters—all movements are in harmony.

1: In the *ai-hanmi* stance.

Make sure that you make a full turn and cut down. If your turn is not complete, your partner can escape, or can be injured during the throw.

Do not attempt to throw your partner out and away. Keep him close to you, otherwise the technique will not work effectively.

5–6: *Tori* makes a turn while controlling *uke*'s wrist with both his hands.

7: *Tori* keeps his hand-swords pressed against *uke*'s shoulder while he steps in and cuts down.

8–10: *Tori* cuts down with both hands and throws *uke*.

2: *Uke* grabs *tori*'s wrist.

3: *Tori* steps in with the back foot and enters as he raises his hand-sword.

4: *Tori* steps in again while raising his hands.

POINT: Harmonize the entering movement and the movement of the hand-sword.

POINT: Make full use of the hand-sword as you enter. Keep your arm close to your body, with a slight bend of the elbow, and full extension of the hand-sword, as you enter as smoothly as possible.

Do not raise your arm away from your ribs.

NAGE-WAZA 4

KATATE-DORI SHIHO-NAGE (URA)
Raise the hand-swords, and cut down through your center

1: In the *gyaku-hanmi* stance.

2

Cut and turn through your center!

5: *Tori* pivots on both feet.

6–9: *Tori* cuts down and throws *uke*.

Cut down straight to your feet. Make a complete turn, and do not attempt to throw your partner out and away. That may result in injury to his elbow or wrist.

Harmonize the movement of the hand-swords and body turn.

In the previous technique, the movement was to the front, but here the movement is to the outside of your partner. In this *ura* technique, *tori* enters to the side of *uke* while raising his hand-sword and turning; he then cuts down to break *uke*'s posture. The entering, turn, and use of the hand-sword must be in harmony. It is very important that the turn is complete, and that you are fully behind your partner.

POINT: Photo 4 from a different angle. Note the full use of the hand-sword harmonized with the body turn.

3–4: As soon as *uke* grabs *tori*'s wrist, *tori* steps in to *uke*'s side, raises his hand-sword, and turns, grabbing *uke*'s arm with both his hands.

As illustrated in photos 3 and 4, keep your body close to your partner's as you turn; if the turn is insufficient, your partner will be too far away to effect the throw.

Cut down and throw your partner through your center!

NAGE-WAZA 5

YOKOMEN-UCHI SHIHO-NAGE (OMOTE)
Against a *yokomen* strike, cut down while simultaneously applying *atemi* to enter and break your partner's posture

1: In the *ai-hanmi* stance.

2: *Uke* delivers a *yokomen* strike.

3–4: As soon as *uke* strikes, *tori* makes a big sweeping turn to the front while cutting down on *uke*'s arm and delivering an *atemi*.

5

6–7

Use *atemi* to break your partner's posture

This technique illustrates well the circular turning movements of Aikido. *Tori* makes a big sweeping turn against a *yokomen* attack, and leads *uke* into a *shiho-nage* throw.

Be careful to cut down on your partner's *yokomen* strike while at the same time delivering an *atemi* and entering. Do not try to block the strike, use a big sweeping turn while cutting down to neutralize the attack. Apply the *atemi* to *uke*'s center.

Atemi is a technique applied to the pressure points of your partner's body to break his posture and neutralize the attack. Here, *atemi* is used for the purpose of breaking your partner's posture.

POINT: Photo 3 from a different angle. Note how *tori* cuts down on *uke*'s arm while delivering an *atemi*.

Apply *atemi* directly to your partner's center.

Cut down on your partner's attacking arm.

A good *atemi* against a *yokomen* strike makes it easy to break your partner's posture.

Cut down as if using a sword when you throw.

8–10: *Tori* cuts down on *uke*'s wrist and throws him.

NAGE-WAZA 6

YOKOMEN-UCHI SHIHO-NAGE (URA)
Harmonize the raising of the hand-swords with the turning movement to lead and throw your partner

1: In the *ai-hanmi* stance.

2–3: As soon as *uke* delivers a *yokomen* strike, *tori* steps in and controls the strike while applying *atemi*.

Photo 3 from a different angle.

Enter to your partner's side and control him with a cut to his arm while applying *atemi* to his face. (This is the same control as that used on the next technique, *tenchi-nage*.)

POINT: Grip your partner's wrist with both hands. Keep his wrist bent and elbow up, and throw him to the back.

Extend your arm and immediately throw your partner.

Here, rather than making a big sweeping turn as on the previous page, you control your partner directly and use an *ura* movement to throw him. Harmonize the cutting motion of the hand-swords with the turning movement.

4–6: *Tori* cuts down on *uke*'s wrist, and then raises his hand-swords as he makes a full turn.

> As illustrated in photos 4–6, harmonize the cutting down and up motions with the turn.

7–9: *Tori* pivots and cuts down to throw *uke*.

71

NAGE-WAZA 7

RYOTE-DORI TENCHI-NAGE
Use the little fingers on both hands to project your power, open across your partner's chest to break his posture

1: In the *ai-hanmi* stance.

2

5–7: *Tori* takes a big step in behind *uke* while cutting down with both hand-swords to throw him.

Use your hand-swords to cut up and down

When you enter, one hand-sword reaches toward heaven and one hand-sword extends toward earth. This breaks your partner's posture and is called *tenchi-nage* (heaven-and-earth throw) in Aikido. The motion of the hand-swords up and down must be harmonized with the entering and throwing movements. You must stay close to your partner, otherwise there will be too great a distance between you and your partner, making it difficult for you to concentrate your power.

3–4: As soon as *uke* grabs both of *tori*'s wrists, *tori* enters to *uke*'s side and simultaneously raises one hand-sword up and one hand-sword down.

As you enter, separate both hand-swords, and extend the upper hand-sword across your partner's chest.

POINT: Be sure to harmonize the up and down motion of the hand-swords with the entering movement. If you only use the hand-swords, it will not be possible to break your partner's posture.

NAGE-WAZA 8

KATATE-DORI UCHI-KAITEN-NAGE
Use your hand-sword to turn inside, get your partner's arm up, and throw him to the front

1: In the *gyaku-hanmi* stance.

2–3: As soon as *uke* grabs *tori*'s wrist, *tori* enters to his side while applying *atemi*.

6–7: *Tori* takes a big step back on his front foot while cutting down with his hand-sword and controlling the back of *uke*'s neck.

8–10: *Tori* grabs *uke*'s wrist, twists *uke*'s body down, and then steps forward to throw him.

POINT 1: The entering *atemi* is very important.
Make sure the *atemi* is strong enough to break your partner's posture, facilitating your turn inward.

POINT 2: Keep your partner's arm straight up.
Make sure your partner's elbow is straight up during the turn and throw. If his arm is horizontal, you will not be able to throw him.

Use *atemi* to enter and turn in the same direction as your partner

In this *kaiten* technique:
—Use your front hand-sword to enter to your partner's side while applying *atemi* with the other hand-sword to break his posture.
—Use *atemi* not from the side but break your partner's posture to the back.
—After the turn, use your hand-sword to raise his arm straight up. If his arm is horizontal, he will be difficult to throw.

4–5: *Tori* takes a big step in with the back foot while raising his hand-sword, and pivots.

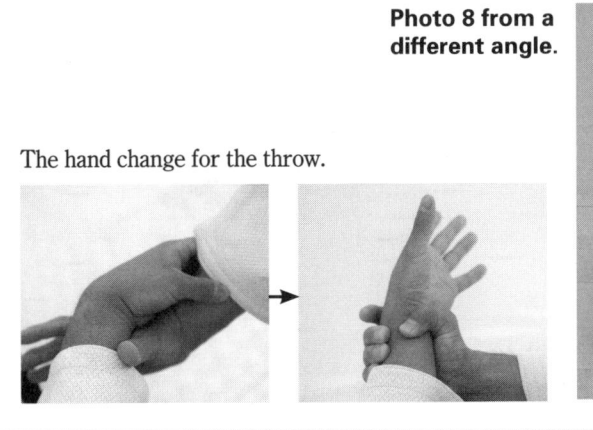

Photo 8 from a different angle.

The hand change for the throw.

NAGE-WAZA 9

KATATE-DORI SOTO-KAITEN-NAGE
Harmonize the entering, the hand-sword, and *atemi* movements

1: In the *gyaku-hanmi* stance.

2–3: As soon as *uke* grabs *tori*'s wrist, *tori* enters to *uke*'s side with *atemi*, and raises his hand-sword.

Photo 4 from a different angle.

While turning to the outside, place your hand-sword in the same direction as your partner.

4–5: While turning, *tori* raises his arm, and then cuts down with his hand-sword while controlling *uke*'s neck.

Do not rely on the strength of your hands and arms alone to move

In the previous example, *uchi-kaiten-nage*, you turned inside of your partner's arm; here, however, you will turn to the outside.

In this technique, note that if you only rely on the strength in your hand and arms when you raise the hand-swords, you will not be able to move smoothly. You need to harmonize the entering move forward, the use of the hand-swords, and the *atemi* as you raise your arms.

POINT: Make full use of the three points when you move. When you raise the arms, make sure that the hand-sword, the movement of the hand-sword, and *atemi* are harmonized.
If the movements are not in unison, you will not be able to raise your arms to apply the technique correctly.

6–8: *Tori* grabs *uke*'s wrist, twists him down, steps forward, and throws him.

KATAME-WAZA 1
AI-HANMI KATATE-DORI DAI-IKKYO (OMOTE)
One knee should be on your partner's side, the other knee on his wrist

1

When you step in with your back foot, do not turn your back to your opponent.

Uke should keep facing *tori* and not turn his back to *tori* until the pin is fully applied.

Uke should go face down flexibly, straight out, without stiffening up.

Uke should use his front hand to take a breakfall. If he keeps his arm back, he will stiffen up and fall badly.

Uke goes face down in the order of arm and knee.

4–5: While controlling *uke*'s elbow, *tori* moves forward and cuts down in an arc.

Use your knees properly to bring your partner to the mat

While moving forward, use your hand-swords to raise and then cut down on your partner's arm and control his elbow and wrist. Pin him face down. This basic technique is known as *dai-ikkyo*.

It is a bit difficult for beginners to work directly from a *shomen-uchi* attack, so we usually start with this kind of reverse grasp attack. In this technique, *tori* follows the main points of *dai-ikkyo* to control his partner flexibly and with a sliding motion.

2–3: As soon as *uke* grabs *tori*'s wrist in an *ai-hanmi* stance, *tori* enters while raising his hand-sword and controls *uke*'s elbow and wrist.

Control your partner's wrist, elbow, and shoulder flexibly. Here, your partner is still facing you.

The inside knee is pinned against your partner's ribs and the outside knee is pinned against his wrist.

6: *Tori* pins *uke* face down by controlling *uke*'s elbow and wrist while he sits up on his toes.

Photo 6 from a different angle.

KATAME-WAZA 2

AI-HANMI KATATE-DORI DAI-IKKYO (URA)
Keep your elbows, shoulders, and hips flexible during the pin, and take the breakfall with your entire body

1

2–3: As soon as *uke* attempts to grab *tori*'s wrist, *tori* raises his hand-sword.

5–6: While making a big turn, *tori* cuts down on *uke*'s arm and pins him face down.

Enter to your partner's side and turn with a big circular movement

This is also a cross-hand technique used for beginners to master the flow of *dai-ikkyo ura* movements. When you turn, your partner must not extend his knees or tighten his shoulders or elbows. Make sure your partner takes the breakfall with his entire body.

Uke should keep his knees flexible and lower himself to the ground naturally with the hips and arms. Both partners need full extension of the body for this technique to work well in practice.

Keep your shoulder, elbow, and wrist flexible.

Keep your knees flexible.

4: *Tori* enters to *uke*'s side while raising his hand-sword and controlling *uke*'s elbow.

Do not keep your arm pulled back.

7 Lower yourself to the mat in the order of hips and hands, making sure not to hit your face on the mat.

8

KATAME-WAZA 3

SHOMEN-UCHI DAI-IKKYO (OMOTE)
Time your movements in harmony with your partner's strike and enter

> Time your movements with your partner's strike and enter.

1: In the *ai-hanmi* stance.

2: As soon as *uke* strikes, *tori* enters to the front while controlling *uke*'s attacking arm.

Extend his arm like this.

Your inner knee should be pressed against his ribs.

Do not let his shoulders float up.

Do not rely only on arm strength, use your entire body to pin him.

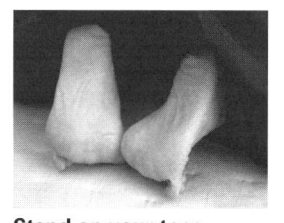

Stand on your toes when you pin.

POINT: The *dai-ikkyo* pin
When your partner is pinned face down, make sure his shoulder cannot float up, and he is directly to his side. Your inner knee should be pressed firmly against his ribs, and the outer knee pressed against his wrist. Do not rely solely on arm strength to pin him but use the entire body to do so. Stand on your toes when you pin.

5: *Tori* moves forward as he controls *uke*'s arm.

Do not let your partner's shoulders float up; enter directly to the side of his body

Time your movements with your partner's *shomen* attack, and control his attacking wrist and elbow with your hand-sword. After controlling his arm, cut down and move forward, breaking your partner's posture and pinning him face down on the mat.

In *dai-ikkyo* be careful to:
—Not let your partner's shoulders float up, but enter directly to his side.
—Pin your partner face down, with you up on your toes. Use your entire body to pin him, not just arm strength.

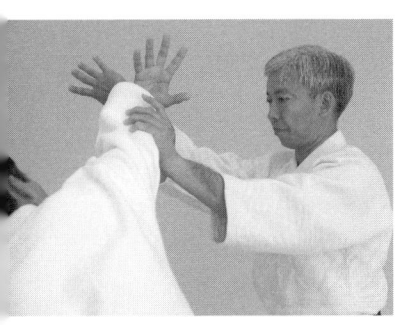

How to control your partner's arm with your hand-sword; do not grab his wrist, use your hand-sword.

3–4: *Tori* controls *uke*'s wrist and elbow as he cuts down.

When entering, cut down on your partner's arm to bring him down; as illustrated in photos 4–7, keep moving forward without stopping.

6–7: *Tori* keeps his back straight, and sits on his toes to pin *uke* face down.

KATAME-WAZA 4
SHOMEN-UCHI DAI-IKKYO (URA)
When turning, bring your partner's elbow to your front

1: In the *ai-hanmi* stance.

2–3: As soon as *uke* delivers a *shomen* strike, *tori* enters to *uke*'s side and controls his elbow and wrist.

4–6: *Tori* makes a big turn while cutting down on *uke*'s arm.

In the *ura* technique a turn is added

Here, a turn is made after your enter to your partner's side. Harmonize your movement with your partner's strike, and enter to his side while you control his elbow and wrist. While turning, cut down on your partner's arm, and pin him face down.

Tori enters to *uke*'s side and controls his elbow and wrist.

Photo 3 from a different angle.

7–8: *Tori* keeps his back straight, controls *uke*'s arm, and pins him face down to the mat.

85

KATAME-WAZA 5

SHOMEN-UCHI DAI-IKKYO SUWARI-WAZA (OMOTE)
Use knee-walking to move forward forcefully, control your partner, and pin him face down

> Coordinate your movements with your partner's attack and enter.

1: In the *seiza* position.

2–4: As soon as *uke* strikes, *tori* moves forward on his knees to *uke*'s inside while controlling his elbow and wrist.

5–6: *Tori* controls *uke*'s elbow and wrist as he cuts down on *uke*'s arm while knee-walking forward.

Knee-walk correctly and keep your center of gravity low

Here, begin from a seated position, sit on the toes, knee-walk forward, and control your partner's movement. This is a valuable training method.

This seated technique is quite similar to the standing version, only performed on the knees. Sit on the toes, and move with your center of gravity low. The key here is to move forcefully from the initial cutting down of your partner's arm to the final pin. Rather than stepping in, as in the standing version, use your knees to move.

As illustrated in photos 5–7, knee-walk forward forcefully to pin your partner face down.

7: *Tori* grabs *uke*'s arm and wrist tightly, and pins him face down.

KATAME-WAZA 6
SHOMEN-UCHI DAI-IKKYO SUWARI-WAZA (URA)
Watch your balance and pivot on the knees

1: Facing each other in *seiza*.

2–3: As soon as *uke* strikes, *tori* enters to *uke*'s outside while controlling his elbow and wrist.

4–7: While pivoting on the knees, *tori* cuts down on *uke*'s arm.

8: *Tori* controls *uke*'s elbow and wrist to pin him face down.

Harmonize the movement of your upper and lower body

In this *ura* technique, the big difference is the pivoting of the knees. Sit on your toes and turn, making sure not to lose your balance. If you lean too far forward, you'll risk losing your balance. Also, when you enter to your partner's side, retain your *hanmi*, and harmonize the movement of the upper and lower parts of your body.

Do not lose your balance.

Keep your partner's elbow in front of you.

POINT: Keep your partner's elbow close to your center as you turn. Harmonize the cutting down of your partner's arm with your turn. During the turn, keep your partner's elbow in front of your center.

89

KATAME-WAZA 7

GYAKU-HANMI KATATE-DORI DAI-IKKYO (OMOTE)
Harmonize your movement with your partner's upward motion and then apply dai-ikkyo

Pay close attention to the timing and distance between you and your partner

Here, we begin in *gyaku-hanmi*—for example, your partner holds your left wrist with his right hand. *Tori* uses *atemi* and a sweeping turn inside to break *uke*'s posture. When your partner attempts to rise, harmonize with that motion, grip his wrist, and control his elbow with your hand-sword while cutting down. Step forward and pin him to the ground. In the practice of this technique, pay attention to the flow of your partner's movement in order to draw him out, and the proper distance and timing.

1

5–6: *Tori* grips *uke*'s wrist and elbow as shown, and controls him.

7–8: *Tori* cuts down on *uke*'s arm while moving forward.

POINT: How to apply the *dai-ikkyo* form and enter
After your partner's posture has been broken by your sweeping turn and *atemi*, harmonize with his attempt to rise, control his wrist, and from there use the *dai-ikkyo* lock to bring him to the mat and pin him.

> Cut down on your partner's arm, do not pull him toward you.

> Use your entire body to cut down, not just your arms.

2–3: As soon as *uke* attempts to grab *tori*'s wrist, *tori* makes a big sweeping motion inside while applying *atemi*.

4: While making a big turn, *tori* cuts down deeply on *uke*'s arm and leads him.

9–10: *Tori* controls *uke*'s elbow and wrist and pins him face down.

> Make sure your partner's posture is completely broken when you grab his wrist.

> Control your partner's wrist with the same hand.

> Control his elbow also as you enter and cut down to pin him.

91

KATAME-WAZA 8

GYAKU-HANMI KATATE-DORI DAI-IKKYO (URA)
While turning your body, keep your center of gravity low while cutting down forcefully with your hand-sword

1

2–3: As soon as *uke* attempts to grab *tori*'s wrist, *tori* enters to *uke*'s outside while applying *atemi*.

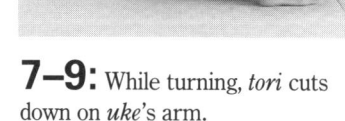

5–6: *Tori* grabs *uke*'s wrist and elbow to control him, and turns.

7–9: While turning, *tori* cuts down on *uke*'s arm.

Use your entire body to cut down, not just your arms

In this *ura* technique, slide to your partner's outside. You must be careful to harmonize the entering movement, the turn, and the cutting down in one well-timed sequence. Again, when cutting down, do not rely on the strength of your arms alone, use your center of gravity to move and control your partner.

> **POINT:** Cut down on your partner's arm while entering. Do not rely on arm strength, use your center of gravity to cut down and break his posture.

4: *Tori* cuts down deeply on *uke*'s arm while entering.

10: *Tori* pins *uke* face down.

KATAME-WAZA 9

SHOMEN-UCHI DAI-NIKYO (OMOTE)
Use the palm of your hand to apply a firm lock on your partner's wrist and control him

1: In the *ai-hanmi* stance.

2: As soon as *uke* strikes, *tori* takes a half-step forward to enter to *uke*'s inside while controlling his arm.

3: While stepping forward, *tori* cuts down on *uke*'s arm.

6–7: *Tori* steps forward.

8: *Tori* gets ready to pin *uke*'s arm.

Dai-nikyo is a training method to strengthen the wrist joints

Training in *dai-nikyo* combines the training in *dai-ikkyo* with strengthening of the elbow, shoulder, and, especially, wrist joints. There is some difference between the *omote* and *ura* versions of the techniques.

Points to watch here are:

—Use the palm of your hand to hold the base of your partner's wrist.

—When pinning your partner on the mat, keep one palm turned up, and the other pressed closely against your partner's elbow.

4–5: *Tori* uses the palm of his hand to grab the base of *uke*'s wrist as shown.

Use the twisting motion of your entire hand to control your partner's lower wrist, making sure to maintain contact throughout.

9: *Tori* pins *uke*'s arm firmly at the elbow and wrist.

Photo 9 shown from a different angle.

KATAME-WAZA 9 (Continued)

POINT 1: How to turn the wrist in *dai-nikyo*
Always maintain contact with your partner's arm, and do not release your grip when you turn your palm. Hold the base of your partner's wrist firmly.

Do not lose contact with your partner's arm.

1

Use the entire palm of your hand to hold the bottom of your partner's wrist firmly.

2

3: Put power in your little finger and hold your partner's wrist firmly.

POINT 2: How to pin in *dai-nikyo*
After your partner is face down, scissor his shoulder with both of your knees, and pin his wrist and elbow with a wrapping motion as shown.

1

2

3: When scissoring your partner's shoulder, one knee should be close to his ribs, and the other knee close to the base of his neck.

4: Use your hand-swords to keep your partner fastened to you.

5: Use your center of gravity to pin your partner. Sit up on your toes.

> Use your knees to scissor his shoulder at his ribs and the base of his neck.

> Keep your top hand-sword with the palm turned up, and the bottom hand-sword pressed against his elbow.

KATAME-WAZA 10

SHOMEN-UCHI DAI-NIKYO (URA)
Lock your partner's lower wrist against your shoulder, and use your center of gravity to control him

1: In the *ai-hanmi* stance.

2–3: As soon as *uke* strikes, *tori* enters to his outside.

As in photos 6 and 7, keep your partner's wrist against your shoulder and apply the lock by moving your center of gravity.

6–7: *Tori* brings *uke*'s wrist against his shoulder and applies a lock.

8–10: *Tori* turns, bringing *uke* face down to the mat, and pins him.

Good and bad examples of *dai-nikyo*

Good example: Draw your partner toward you when applying the *nikyo* lock. As in photo 3, you should be facing each other, and be well centered. ○

1 2 3 4

Use the correct grip in *dai-nikyo*

In this technique it is important to control your partner's lower wrist in the correct manner. Furthermore, after the lock to the wrist is applied to your shoulder, the movement of your center of gravity is used to control and bring your partner down.

4–5: While turning, *tori* cuts down on *uke*'s arm and switches to the *dai-nikyo* grip.

Bad example: Your partner is facing away from you when you attempt the lock, and it turns into an elbow technique, not what was intended. ✗

1   **2**

KATAME-WAZA 11
KATA-DORI DAI-NIKYO (OMOTE)
During the big sweeping turn, do not pull on your partner's arm

1: In the *gyaku-hanmi* stance.

2

POINT: When you place the lock on your partner's wrist, keep it against your shoulder. Do not use just your hands to apply the lock but your shoulders as well.

6–8: *Tori* applies the *nikyo* lock to *uke*'s wrist, and cuts down on his arm while moving forward.

Harmonize the sweeping turn movement with the cutting down of the hand-sword

This is a technique for when your partner grabs your shoulder. As soon as he attempts to grab, make a big sweeping turn while applying *atemi* to break his posture. Cut down deeply on his lower wrist, apply the *nikyo* lock, and cut down again on his arm while moving forward to pin him face down.

The main points here are not to pull your partner's arm when you make the sweeping turn. Also, you must harmonize your turning movements with the cutting down of the hand-sword.

> As in photos 4–5, harmonize your movement with the cutting down of the sword.

3: As soon as *uke* attempts to grab *tori*'s shoulder, *tori* applies *atemi*.

4–5: While making a sweeping turn, *tori* cuts down on *uke*'s arm.

> As illustrated in photos 4 and 5, use a big sweeping turn to break your partner's posture, do not pull his arm. Also, when making the turn and cutting down on his arm, do not lose your own balance.

9–10: *Tori* pins *uke* face down with *nikyo*.

KATAME-WAZA 12

KATA-DORI DAI-NIKYO (URA)
Lock your partner's wrist against your shoulder and use your entire body to pin him

1: In the *gyaku-hanmi* stance.

2–3: As soon as *uke* attempts to grab *tori*'s shoulder, *tori* applies *atemi* while entering.

Make your movement and the cutting down with the hand-sword in one fluid motion.

5–6: *Tori* applies the *nikyo* grip on *uke*'s arm while turning and cutting down.

9–12: While turning, *tori* controls *uke*, brings him face down on the mat, and pins him.

Harmonize your body movement and the cutting down of the hand-sword

In the previous *omote* technique, there was a sweeping turn to the inside, but in this *ura* technique the movement and pin are diagonal to the back. As in the *omote* technique, harmonize the movement of your body with the cutting down of the hand-sword in a smooth flowing motion. Also, when you apply the *nikyo* lock, keep your partner's wrist firmly against your shoulder and use your entire body to pin him.

Do not pull your partner's arm, cut down low on it.

4: *Tori* cuts down on *uke*'s arm from the outside.

Lock your partner's wrist firmly against your shoulder and pin him with your entire body.

7–8: *Tori* places *uke*'s wrist against his shoulder and applies the lock.

103

KATAME-WAZA 13

SHOMEN-UCHI DAI-SANKYO
When applying the *dai-sankyo* lock, grip your partner's palm and thrust up

1: In the *ai-hanmi* stance.

2: As soon as *uke* strikes, *tori* enters.

5–6: *Tori* grips *uke*'s palm and thrusts it upward.

7–8: *Tori* switches his grip, and applies the *dai-sankyo* lock to *uke*'s wrist.

Take care with the grip, the lock, and the pin

Dai-sankyo is an arm pin like *dai-ikkyo*, but a different way to lock and pin your partner's wrist than *dai-nikyo*. It stimulates a different set of muscles.

In *dai-sankyo*:
—Apply the lock, the entry, and the turn correctly.
—Pin your partner face down.
—Switch your grip when you pin his arm.

3–4: *Tori* controls *uke*'s elbow and wrist, and cuts down on his arm while moving forward.

9: *Tori* steps forward on the back foot, and immediately pivots, controlling *uke*'s arm.

10–11: *Tori* pivots and steps back while cutting down on *uke*'s arm.

12–13: *Tori* brings *uke* face down to the mat and pins him.

KATAME-WAZA 13 (Continued)

POINT 1: How to apply the *dai-sankyo* lock
In order to apply the *dai-sankyo* lock smoothly, turn the palm of your partner's hand and thrust up, and then change hands from underneath.

Turn your partner's palm and thrust up.	The hand that was controlling his elbow is now used to grasp his palm from underneath, and apply the *dai-sankyo* lock.	With the lock in place, cut down and bring your partner's shoulder and elbow to a low position.

POINT 3: Pin with *dai-sankyo*
In the *dai-sankyo* arm pin, use the arm that was controlling your partner's elbow to grab his wrist deep to the inside and change your grip, making sure that your partner's shoulder is firmly scissored by your knees. After the grip change, your partner's wrist should be firmly turned against your chest with one hand, and the other hand pressed palm up against his elbow.

POINT 2: How to bring your partner down in *dai-sankyo*
In order to move smoothly from the *dai-sankyo* lock to the *dai-sankyo* pin, you have to turn properly and cut down. If you execute this movement correctly, your partner's head, shoulder, and elbow will be in a straight line.

1: Take one step forward.

2: Control your partner's elbow.

3: Pivot on your front foot, bringing your partner's head forward.

4: Take a step back and sit down, bringing your partner all the way down to the front.

Twist his wrist, and pin his shoulders firmly.

This hand should have the palm up, and you should pin against his side.

The hand controlling your partner's elbow should be used to hold and twist the inside of his wrist.

KATAME-WAZA 14

SHOMEN-UCHI DAI-SANKYO (URA)
When you apply the *dai-sankyo* lock, make sure you are on your partner's outside

1: In the *ai-hanmi* stance.

2: As soon as *uke* strikes, *tori* enters to *uke*'s outside and controls his elbow and wrist.

3–4: While turning, *tori* cuts down on *uke*'s arm.

As in photos 7–9, bring your partner's arm by cutting through your center.

7–8: While turning, *tori* controls *uke*'s elbow and cuts down.

9–11: *Tori* brings *uke* face down to the mat, changes his grip, and pins *uke* firmly in *dai-sankyo*.

Cut down on your partner's arm through your center

In this *ura* version of *dai-sankyo*, the lock and pin are applied similarly but with a circular motion. After the initial turn, there is one more entry and a turn while cutting down on your partner's arm to bring him to the ground.

Important points:
—When you apply the *dai-sankyo* lock, make sure you are to *uke*'s outside.
—When cutting down on your partner's arm, do so through your own center.

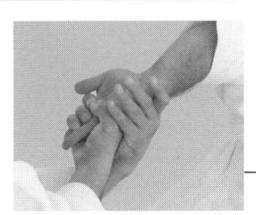

5: *Tori* applies the *dai-sankyo* lock to *uke*'s wrist, with his palm upturned, and an upward thrusting motion.

Enter to your partner's side and apply the *dai-sankyo* lock.

6: While applying the *dai-sankyo* lock, *tori* enters to *uke*'s outside.

KATAME-WAZA 15

SHOMEN-UCHI DAI-YONKYO (OMOTE)
Concentrate your power in the base of your index finger, and pin your partner by applying that pressure to his pulse.

1: In the *ai-hanmi* stance.

2–3: As soon as *uke* strikes, *tori* uses his handswords to control the attacking arm.

POINT: How to apply the *dai-yonkyo* lock and pin
Apply pressure to your partner's pulse with the base of your index finger. Keep your partner's arm firmly against your body to pin him.

Use both your hands to pin him, and stay close to his body.

Use your entire body to pin your partner, not just arm strength.

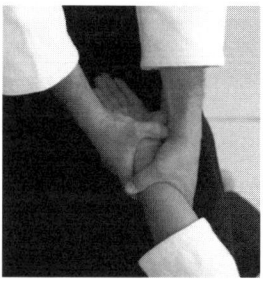

Concentrate your power at the base of your index finger, and you can pin him smoothly.

Do not apply pressure with just your grip, but use your entire body

Here, in addition to the *dai-ikkyo* arm pin, pressure is applied to the weak point of the wrist. This is another method of training. In this technique, pressure is not applied to the joints, but to the weak spots on the inner and outer wrist. Apply pressure to your partner's wrist with the base of your index finger and use that pressure together with the force of your entire body to pin him.

> Push forward on your partner's extended arm in order to pin him more easily.

4: While stepping forward, *tori* uses both hand-swords to cut down on *uke*'s wrists.

5: *Tori* keeps moving forward, bringing *uke* down to the mat.

6–8: *Tori* grips *uke*'s pulse and applies pressure with the base of his index finger in the *dai-yonkyo* lock to pin him.

111

KATAME-WAZA 16
SHOMEN-UCHI DAI-YONKYO (URA)
Concentrate your power at the base of your index finger, and apply pressure to the outside pulse of your partner

1: In the *ai-hanmi* stance.

2: As soon as *uke* strikes, *tori* enters to *uke*'s side and controls his elbow and wrist.

6: *Tori* applies the *dai-yonkyo* lock to *uke*'s outside pulse with an upward thrust.

7–9: While turning, *tori* cuts all the way down on *uke*'s arm, bringing him to the mat.

10: *Tori* brings *uke* face down to the mat while applying the *dai-yonkyo* lock to pin him.

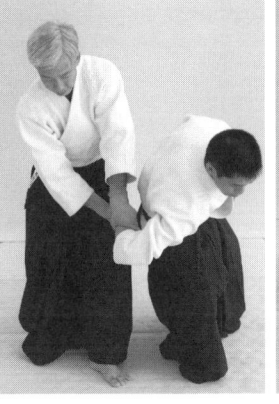

Photo 10 from a different angle.

Use your center of gravity to control your partner's shoulder

This is the same *dai-yonkyo* lock as the previous example, but applied to the outside pulse of your partner's wrist. The location of this outside pulse is somewhat harder to find than the inside pulse, so some care is needed. Use your center of gravity as well as the *dai-yonkyo* grip to apply the pin.

3

4–5: While turning, *tori* cuts down on *uke*'s arm.

POINT: How to apply the *dai-yonkyo* lock and pin in the *ura* technique

Lock

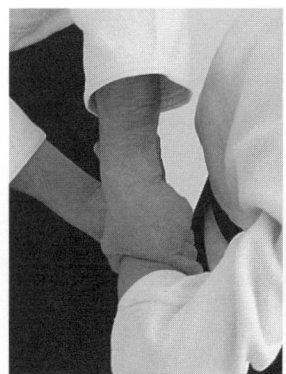

Shift the hand that was controlling your partner's elbow to his outside pulse.

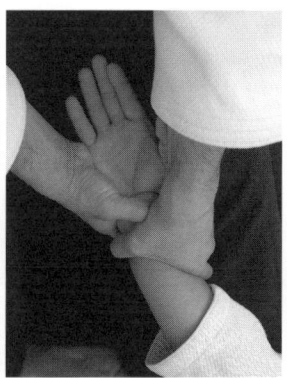

Concentrate your power at the base of your index finger to apply the lock.

Pin

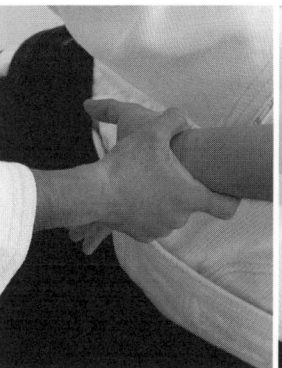

Apply the base of your index finger to your partner's outside pulse, and use your entire body to pin him.

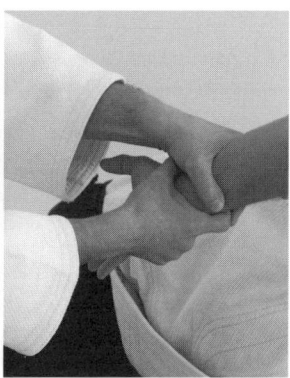

Keep your hands in close proximity; it is easier to pin your partner if his elbow is slightly bent.

NAGE-KATAME-WAZA 1

SHOMEN-UCHI KOTE-GAESHI
When applying the *kote-gaeshi* grip, hold the hand firmly with no break in continuity

1: In the *ai-hanmi* stance.

2–3: As soon as *uke* delivers a strike, *tori* enters to *uke*'s outside and cuts down on his arm while turning.

POINT 1: Hold the outside of your partner's hand firmly, with no break in continuity, and no separation.

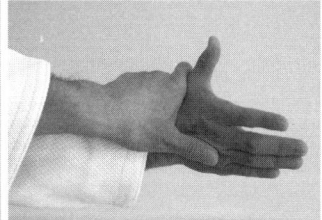

5–7: *Tori* applies the *kote-gaeshi* lock to *uke*'s hand while turning and leading him.

10–14: *Tori* pins *uke* face down as shown.

As illustrated in photos 10–12, keep your body well centered as your turn your partner face over.

Use the entering movement and turn to completely break your partner's posture

In this technique, a throw is combined with a pin. Neutralize your partner's attack with a good entry and flowing movement, and then apply a lock to his joints and pin him face down.

In *shomen-uchi kote-gaeshi*, apply a lock to the back of your partner's hand to throw him. Do not rely on that lock alone, but use the entering, turning, and foot movements to completely break his posture.

POINT 2: When applying the *kote-gaeshi* lock, harmonize your body movements and cut down through your center.

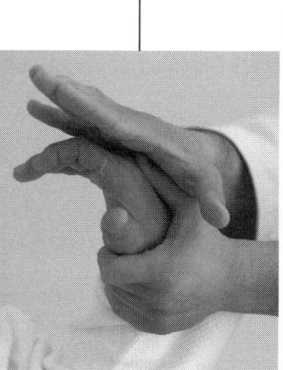

Do not try to throw your partner far out; throw him to your front.

8–9: *Tori* keeps moving while applying the *kote-gaeshi* lock, cuts down, and throws *uke*.

115

NAGE-KATAME-WAZA 2
KATATE-DORI KOTE-GAESHI
Make full use of your hand-swords to break your partner's grip

1: In the *gyaku-hanmi* stance.

2–3: As soon as *uke* attempts to grab *tori*'s wrist, *tori* enters and turns, using his hand-swords to scissor *uke*'s hand.

6–9: While turning, *tori* leads *uke* down and throws him.

10–12: *Tori* pins *uke* face down.

Do not let your freed hand-sword lose contact with your partner's hand

In this *katate-dori kote-gaeshi* technique, make full use of both hand-swords to break your partner's grip on your wrist. Then turn, break his posture, throw him with a wrist turn, and pin him face down.

When using both hand-swords, be sure that the freed hand-sword remains in contact with the outside of your partner's hand. Also, it is important to keep that hand close to his arm while applying the *kote-gaeshi* grip.

4–5: *Tori* releases *uke*'s grip and uses his freed hand-sword to grab *uke*'s hand with the *kote-gaeshi* lock.

POINT: Make full use of your hand-swords to break your partner's grip. When you want to break your partner's grip on your wrist, do not use just the cutting hand-sword, use the hand-sword that is being held as well, moving it into the space between his thumb and index finger.

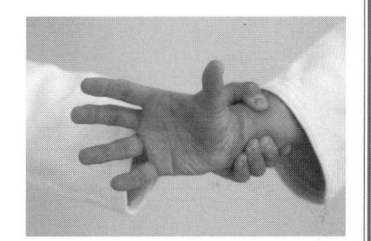

1: Your partner holds your wrist.

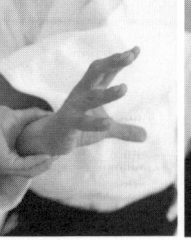

Scissor his hand.

Use the motion of both hand-swords to break his grip.

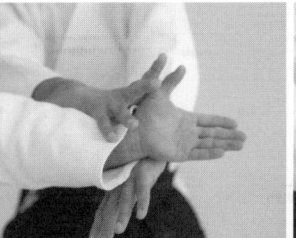

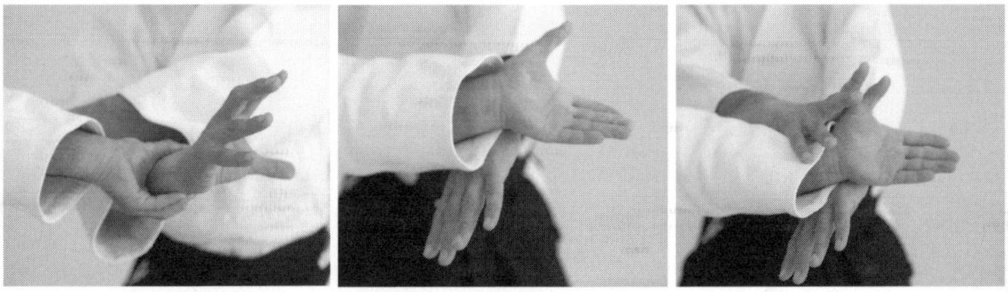

Do not let the freed hand-sword lose contact with his arm.

2–4: Turn your held hand-sword inward as you use your other hand-sword to scissor his hand, thus breaking his grip.

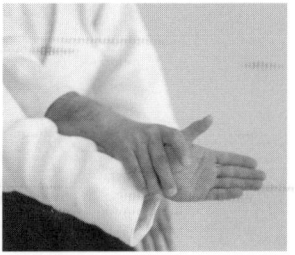

5: After breaking his grip, keep the freed hand-sword against his arm.

NAGE-KATAME-WAZA 3

TSUKI KOTE-GAESHI
Against a thrusting attack you must turn with a forceful movement

1: In the *ai-hanmi* stance.

2–3: As soon as *uke* thrusts, *tori* enters to *uke*'s outside and applies the *kote-gaeshi* lock to his hand.

4–5: *Tori* applies the *kote-gaeshi* lock and turns, leading *uke*.

9–11: *Tori* pins *uke* face down and applies a finishing armlock.

Use a turn to break your partner's posture, and then throw him with *kote-gaeshi*

Against a thrusting attack, in this *tsuki kote-gaeshi* technique, control your partner's arm with your hand-sword, enter and turn to break his posture and throw him, and then pin him face down. It is important to enter and turn smoothly around his thrust to break his posture and down him.

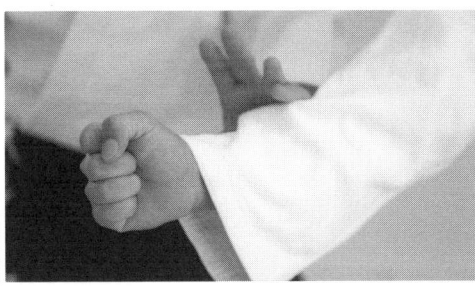

In order to control your partner's wrist in subsequent movements, it is very important to enter cleanly, completely avoiding his thrust.

6–8: *Tori* takes a wide step and throws *uke* with *kote-gaeshi*.

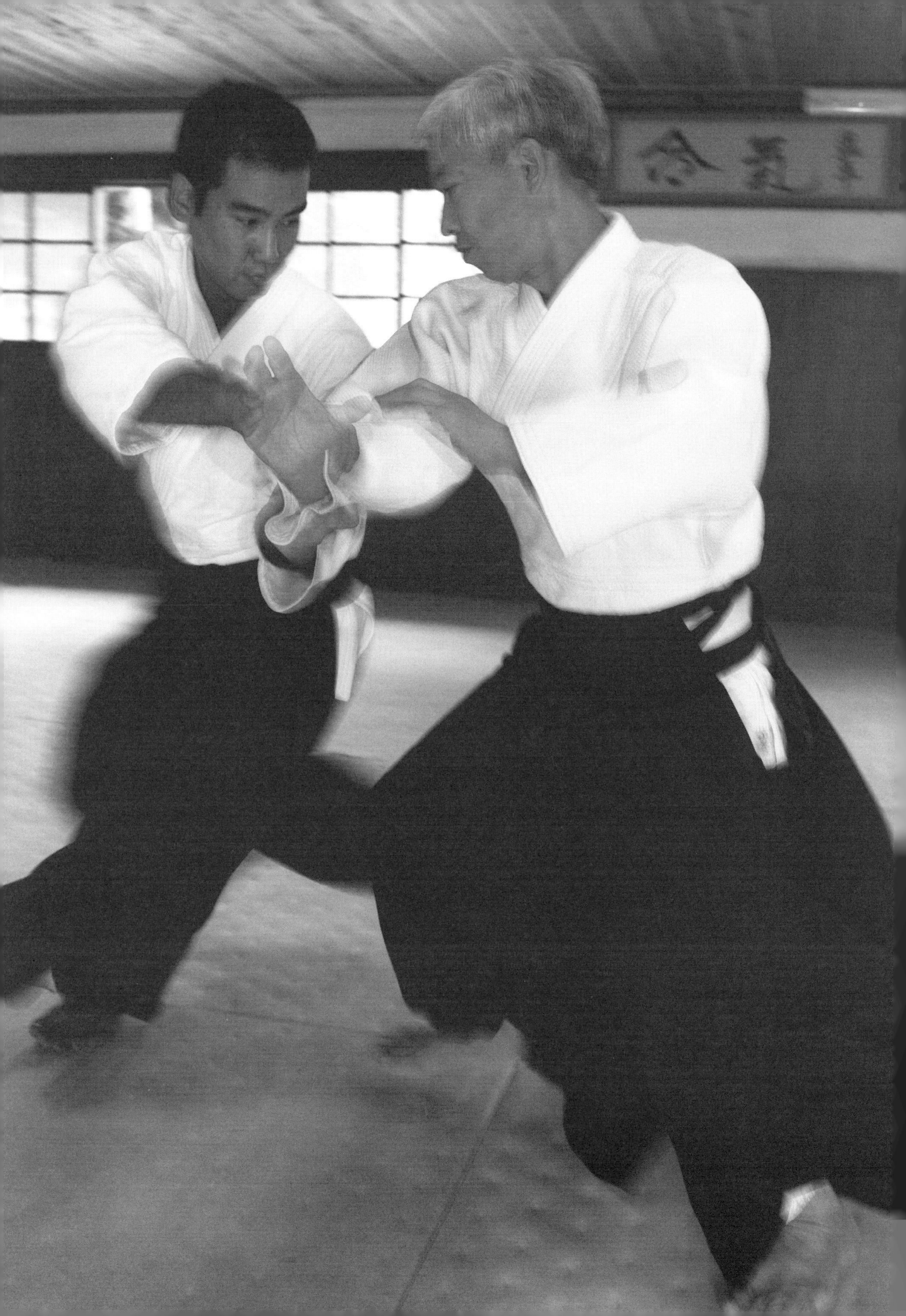

CHAPTER 4

Acquiring Skill in Basic Variations

NAGE-WAZA 1

YOKOMEN-UCHI IRIMI-NAGE
Make the sweeping turn, the use of your hand-swords, and the entering movements as smoothly as possible

Use your hand-sword in a sweeping cut to make your entry easier

In *yokomen-uchi irimi-nage* you control your partner's attacking *yokomen* strike while making a sweeping turn; sweep his arm with your hand-sword, enter and turn, and break his posture to throw him.

The key here is to keep in motion during the entry and the turn, and not become inert.
— Make a sweeping turn while cutting down against your partner's *yokomen* attack.
— Make a sweeping cut on his attacking arm to enter to his side, and face the same direction.
— Enter to your partner's side while controlling his neck.

Perform all three of these actions in a smooth flow, free of breaks.

1: In the *ai-hanmi* stance.

4–6: *Tori* uses his *atemi* hand-sword to make a sweeping cut on *uke*'s arm, enters to his outside, and controls his neck.

POINT: Make a sweeping turn while cutting down on your partner's arm, and then use your hand-sword to make a sweeping cut to enter. If you do not do this in a smooth flow, it will be difficult to lead your partner.

Make the sweeping turn and the movement of your hand-swords together in one flowing motion.

Direction of the sweeping turn.

1: Control your partner's attack with your hand-sword while making a sweeping turn and cutting down.

2: Use your hand-sword to make a sweeping cut to your partner's arm.

2–3: As soon as *uke* strikes, *tori* applies *atemi* while making a big sweeping turn to the inside, cuts down on *uke*'s arm, and leads him.

7–9: *Tori* steps forward while cutting down to throw *uke*.

Make a sweeping cut with your hand-sword.

Direction of entry.

3: After the sweeping cut, face the same direction as your partner, facilitating the entry to his side.

4: Enter to your partner's side.

5: Turn to lead your partner.

123

NAGE-WAZA 2
HANMI-HANTACHI KATATE-DORI SHIHO-NAGE
In seated throws make full use of your feet to enter and turn

Harmonize your entry and the movement of your hand-swords

Here, your partner attacks from a standing position while you remain seated. Your partner grabs your wrist from above and you employ a *shiho-nage* throw.

Important points are:
—Do not rely on arm strength alone when you raise your hand-swords; use the entire power of your movement forward.
—When you make the cutting turn, do not lose your balance, and turn quickly in a big movement.
—When throwing from a seated position, do not extend your partner's arm outward; use your body turn to bring him down close to your knee.

1: *Uke* stands diagonally in front of *tori*, who sits in *seiza*.

As illustrated in photos 4–8, do not extend your partner's arm outward; throw him by making a body turn and cutting down close to your knee.

4–8: *Tori* cuts down on *uke*'s wrist while sliding forward, and throws him.

When you make the turn, do not lose your balance, and move quickly with a big movement. If you only turn halfway you will not be able to throw your partner well.

The power of movement forward

The power of raised hand-sword

2–3: As soon as *uke* attempts to grab *tori*'s wrist, *tori* enters to *uke*'s inside while raising his hand-sword.

Harmonize your movement forward with the raising of your hand-sword. If you rely only on the power of your hand-sword you will not move well.

NAGE-WAZA 3
HANMI-HANTACHI RYOTE-DORI SHIHO-NAGE (OMOTE)
Step forward deeply under your partner's arm as if lifting him up

1: *Uke* is standing, *tori* faces him in *seiza*.

2: *Uke* grabs both of *tori*'s wrists from the front.

5–7: *Tori* takes a step forward while cutting down on *uke*'s wrist to throw him.

Make a big turn to face in the opposite direction

Here your partner grabs both wrists from the front. This attack is very strong, so you need much bigger movements than in the previous example of one hand held. It is important that you step in deeply as if lifting your partner's arm. If your movement is too shallow, you will be blocked by your partner's arm when you stand. Be sure to be turned in the direction of your partner's back and cut down correctly.

> Use the power of the entering (forward) movement and your lower body to raise your arms.

> Make sure that you are facing your partner's back after the turn.

3: *Tori* uses his hand-swords to lead *uke*.

4: *Tori* raises his hand-swords and turns.

> **POINT:** Enter deeply as if raising your partner's arms. If your entry is too shallow, you will be blocked by your partner's arms when you try to stand.

NAGE-WAZA 4

HANMI-HANTACHI RYOTE-DORI SHIHO-NAGE (URA)
Pivot on your entering foot while keeping your center of gravity low

1: *Uke* is standing, *tori* faces him in *seiza*.

2

> Move your arms and body in a direct line.

5: *Tori* leads both of *uke*'s wrists as he stands all the way up.

6: While rotating his hand-swords, *tori* makes a full turn.

7–9: *Tori* steps forward, cuts down, and throws *uke*.

Make a big turn to effect the throw

In this *ura* technique, use the front foot as a pivot when you turn, and keep your center of gravity low. If this foot is not stable, you will not be able to pivot well, and will be likely to lose your balance halfway. Be sure that you make a full turn and be facing your partner's back when you finish.

> Move as soon as your partner grabs your wrists.

> Keep your center of gravity in the front foot. When you stand and turn, this foot will be your pivot.

3–4: As soon as *uke* attempts to grab *tori*'s wrists, *tori* enters to *uke*'s outside.

NAGE-WAZA 5

SHOMEN-UCHI KAITEN-NAGE
Enter directly to your partner's outside smoothly, avoiding his attack

Control your partner's lower neck and wrist to throw him in *kaiten-nage*

In this technique, control your partner's *shomen* attack by holding his wrist and the back of his neck while turning in *kaiten-nage*. Harmonize your initial entering movement with your partner's attack, and enter directly—this is important. If you do not enter directly all the way to your partner's side, you will break the flow of the technique.

1: In the *ai-hanmi* stance.

5: *Tori* grabs *uke*'s wrist, and twists him down.

POINT:
It is crucial to enter directly to your partner's outside as soon as he attacks. If you do not, it will be very difficult to counter the attack. Also, be sure to use the correct grip on your partner's wrist and lower neck when you cut down.

1: As soon as your partner attacks, enter directly; if you do not enter deeply enough you cannot control his arm.

Press down on your partner's lower neck to break his posture.

Control his wrist and pull it back.

2: Harmonize the movements against your partner's wrist and lower neck to break his posture.

2–3: As soon as *uke* strikes, *tori* enters to *uke*'s outside.

3–4: *Tori* cuts down on *uke*'s wrist while controlling the bottom of his neck.

6–7: *Tori* steps forward and throws *uke*.

When pulling his arm back use his trapped wrist.

3: After pressing his lower neck all the way down, correctly hold his wrist.

4: Push down on your partner's lower neck, and twist him in.

KATAME-WAZA 1

YOKOMEN-UCHI DAI-IKKYO (OMOTE)
Use your hand-sword to slide up on your partner's arm, and then cut down while controlling his elbow

1: In the *ai-hanmi* stance.

2: As soon as *uke* strikes, *tori* raises his arms.

6–8: *Tori* slides his hand-sword up, raising *uke*'s arm, and then cuts down on that arm while controlling *uke*'s elbow and moving forward.

POINT: Use your hand-sword to slide your partner's arm up and down.

From the *atemi* to the final pin, use your hand-sword in a sliding motion to move your partner's arm up and down while controlling his elbow.

1: Place your *atemi* hand-sword under your partner's wrist after cutting down.

Make the cutting change correctly

In this *yokomen-uchi dai-ikkyo* technique, you neutralize your partner's *yokomen* attack with a sweeping turn while applying *atemi*, slide his attacking arm up, and then cut down to pin him on the mat.

The most important point here is to make the transition of the hand-swords correctly. Use your *atemi* hand-sword to slide his arm and control his elbow with the other hand-sword with a smooth crossover movement. If this is done correctly, you will be able to break your partner's posture, and then cut down and pin him smoothly.

3–4: *Tori* enters to *uke*'s inside while making a sweeping turn and applying *atemi*.

5: *Tori* cuts down deeply on *uke*'s attacking arm and leads him.

9–10: *Tori* pins *uke* face down.

2–3: Slide your front hand-sword up raising your partner's arm.

4: Control his elbow.

KATAME-WAZA 2

YOKOMEN-UCHI DAI-IKKYO (URA)
Harmonize the use of your hand-swords and the turning movement in a smooth flow

1: In the *ai-hanmi* stance.

2–3: As soon as *uke* strikes, *tori* enters to *uke*'s outside while controlling the attacking arm with one hand-sword and applying *atemi* with the other.

6–8: *Tori* cuts down on *uke*'s arm while turning.

POINT: The switching of hand-swords after the entry

After entering to your partner's side, the hand-sword change and elbow control is the same as that in the *omote* technique, but an immediate turn is made while you cut down on your partner's arm. If the hand-sword change and the turn are not made in unison, the flow of the technique will be broken.

1: Enter and control your partner's *yokomen* strike with one hand-sword while applying *atemi* with the other.

2: Place the *atemi* hand-sword under your partner's wrist.

Use your hand-sword to slide your partner's arm up, control his elbow, and then cut down

Unlike the previous technique, which employed a sweeping turn inside, in this *ura* technique, you enter to your partner's outside while applying *atemi*, switch your hand-swords, and turn. The hand-sword change and elbow control is the same as in the *omote* technique, but here an immediate turn to the outside is added. If the use of the hand-swords and the turning movement are not harmonized, the flow of the technique will be broken and your movement jerky.

4–5: *Tori* slides *uke*'s arm up while controlling his elbow.

9–10: *Tori* pins *uke* face down on the mat.

3: Slide up on your partner's arm while controlling his elbow.

4–5: While turning, cut down on your partner's arm. In photos 1–5, notice the smooth flow of the transition.

KATAME-WAZA 3

MOROTE-DORI DAI-NIKYO (OMOTE)
Raise your hand-sword while moving your feet diagonally to the front

1: In the *gyaku-hanmi* stance.

2–3: *Uke* steps in and grabs *tori*'s arm with both of his hands.

5–6: While cutting down on *uke*'s arm, *tori* applies the *dai-nikyo* lock to his wrist.

6–7: *Tori* brings *uke* face down to the mat and pins him with *dai-nikyo*.

When your partner grabs your arm with both of his hands

When your partner grabs one of your arms with both of his hands it is called *morote-dori*. In this *dai-nikyo* technique, make full use of your hand-swords when your partner grabs you while moving forward to apply the *dai-nikyo* lock. Break your partner's posture by opening to the side and making full use of your hand-swords while moving smoothly.

> Harmonize the forward movement with the raising of your hand-swords.

4: *Tori* opens diagonally to the front while raising his hand swords, and controls *uke*'s elbow.

8

TERMINOLOGY

morote-dori: When your partner grabs one of your arms with both of his hands.

ryote-dori: When your partner grabs both of your arms. When he grabs both of your wrists it is called *ryotekubi-dori*.

KATAME-WAZA 4

MOROTE-DORI DAI-NIKYO (URA)
Harmonize your body movement with the cutting down of the hand-sword to apply the lock

1: In the *gyaku-hanmi* stance.

2

> Be sure to bend your partner's elbow, or the *dai-nikyo* lock will not be effective.

5–6: While turning, *tori* cuts down and applies the *dai-nikyo* lock to *uke*'s wrist.

7–8: While still turning, *tori* cuts down on *uke*'s arm.

POINT: Before applying the *dai-nikyo* lock, use the motion of your hand-sword to bend your partner's arm. If his arm is straight the *dai-nikyo* lock will not work. If his arm is not bent you need to apply an elbow lock variation.

Use the motion of your hand-sword to bend your partner's elbow

In this *morote-dori nikyo* technique, harmonize the turning of your body and the use of the hand-swords to lock and pin your partner's hand-sword. When you apply the *dai-nikyo* lock it is important to use the motion of your hand-sword to bend your partner's elbow. Do not let your partner escape your grip, and use both of your hands to apply the lock.

3–4: As soon as *uke* attempts to grab *tori*'s arm with both wrists, *tori* enters to *uke*'s outside while raising his arms and applying the *dai-nikyo* lock to his wrist.

Be sure to control your partner's wrist with the hand and hand-sword; if you do not, your partner can easily escape the following cut down.

9–10: *Tori* brings *uke* face down to the mat and pins him with *dai-nikyo*.

Use your hand-sword to cut in and down deeply.

Harmonize the bending of your partner's elbow with the cutting down of your hand-sword.

Do not let your elbows rise.

139

KATAME-WAZA 5

USHIRO RYOTEKUBI-DORI DAI-SANKYO (OMOTE)
As if placing your partner's chest up on your back, raise your hand-swords and draw him out

1: In the *ai-hanmi* stance.

2–4: *Uke* cuts down on *tori*'s hand-sword while moving behind *tori* to grab both of his wrists.

6: *Tori* steps back on the front foot, and applies the *dai-sankyo* lock to *uke*'s wrist.

Photo 6 from a different angle.

Keep the *dai-sankyo* lock on *uke*'s wrist throughout the exercise.

7–10: While continuing to apply the *dai-sankyo* lock, *tori* cuts down on *uke*'s elbow while turning.

11–12: *Tori* takes another step back while cutting with his hand-sword, brings *uke* face down to the mat, and pins him down with *dai-sankyo*.

Let your partner grasp your wrists tightly

This technique is used when your partner has grasped your wrists tightly from behind. Circular, spiral movements of the hand-swords are the bases of this technique. When your partner grabs your wrists from behind, raise your hand-swords high, imagining his chest pressing close to your back. Your partner must hold your wrists tightly; if he lets go you cannot practice this technique correctly.

5: *Tori* raises his hand-swords.

POINT: How to raise the hand-swords

When held tightly by both wrists from behind, raise your arms, bringing your partner's chest up on your back.

Your partner grabs your wrists firmly from behind.

Make sure your partner maintains a tight hold of your wrists; this is essential for correct practice.

Bring your partner's chest close to your back by raising your hand-swords.

KATAME-WAZA 6
USHIRO RYOTEKUBI-DORI DAI-SANKYO (URA)
Enter to your partner's side and apply *dai-sankyo*

1: In the *ai-hanmi* stance.

2–3: *Uke* cuts down on *tori*'s wrist and grabs *tori*'s wrists from behind.

5–6: *Tori* steps back with the front foot while cutting down with both hand-swords, and applies the *dai-sankyo* lock to *uke*'s wrist.

10

11

Use the breath power of both hand-swords to break your partner's posture

In the *ura* version of this technique, first raise both hand-swords and then cut down while entering to your partner's side. Turn to break his posture, bring him face down to the mat, and pin him. This *ura* technique has many things in common with the *omote* version, but the *dai-sankyo* lock is applied to the inside of your partner's arm, so do not let him get too far away. In short, the *omote* version is move to the front and turn, the *ura* version is move to the side and turn.

4: *Tori* raises both hand-swords.

7–8: *Tori* controls *uke*'s elbow while turning and entering to *uke*'s side.

8–11: *Tori* keeps turning while cutting down on *uke*'s arm. *Tori* pins *uke* face down on the mat, presses *uke*'s hand-sword against his chest, binds his arm, and pins him.

> Be sure to apply the *dai-sankyo* lock to your partner's wrist while you are to his side; if he moves away from you, you cannot apply the pin.

KATAME-WAZA 7

YOKOMEN-UCHI DAI-YONKYO (OMOTE)
Cut down while making a big sweeping turn in a smooth motion, and completely lead your partner

Control your partner's *yokomen* strike with your hand-swords, and lead him firmly

In this *yokomen-uchi dai-yonkyo* technique, you lead your partner by making a sweeping turn inside while cutting down on his attacking arm. Then you use your hand-sword to slide up your partner's arm, then cut down to break his posture, and pin him face down while applying the *dai-yonkyo* lock. The key here is making the sweeping turn and cutting down smoothly to lead your partner in one continuous flow. If you do not lead him completely, the distance will be too great and you will not be able to lead him into the next technical sequence. Harmonize the motion of the hand-swords and the sweeping turn in order to fully lead your partner.

1: In the *ai-hanmi* stance.

4: While making a sweeping turn, *tori* cuts down on *uke*'s arm to lead him.

5–6: *Tori* slides his hand-sword up *uke*'s arm while controlling his elbow.

9–10: *Tori* pins *uke* face down on the mat while applying the *dai-yonkyo* pin to his wrist.

As in photos 3–4, make the *atemi,* the entering sweep, and the leading of your partner in one smooth flow. If you do not, you will not be able to control him properly in the following movement because the distance will be too great.

Cut down forcibly on *uke*'s attacking arm.

Sweeping turn direction.

2–3: As soon as *uke* strikes, *tori* enters to *uke*'s inside while applying *atemi* and making a big sweeping turn.

7–8: *Tori* cuts down on *uke*'s arm while moving forward.

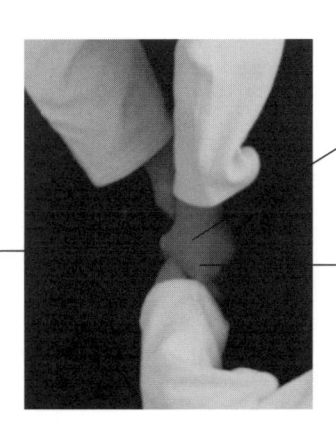

Apply the lock to his pulse.

Concentrate your power in the base of your index finger and use your entire body to apply pressure to his pulse.

KATAME-WAZA 8

YOKOMEN-UCHI DAI-YONKYO (URA)
Bring your partner down low and then apply the *dai-yonkyo* lock

1: In the *ai-hanmi* stance.

2–3: As soon as *uke* attacks, *tori* enters to *uke*'s outside while applying *atemi* and controlling *uke*'s attacking arm.

5: *Tori* cuts down on *uke*'s right arm while turning.

6: *Tori* applies the *dai-yonkyo* lock to the outside of *uke*'s wrist, and makes a thrust up on *uke*'s arm.

> Apply the *dai-yonkyo* lock shift of hands to your partner's side.

Shift your grip to apply *dai-yonkyo* to the outside of your partner's grip

The key point in this *ura* technique is to cut down low on your partner's arm, bringing his body low, and then applying the *dai-yonkyo* lock. If the application of the lock is too high, your partner can easily counter the attack. Be sure to make the shift in grip from your partner's outside.

Enter deeply against *yokomen* attacks.

4: *Tori* slides his hand-sword up *uke*'s arm while controlling his elbow.

7–9: *Tori* continues to cut down, bringing *uke* face down to the mat. *Tori* pins *uke* with *dai-yonkyo*.

Use your entire body to apply pressure in the pin.

10

147

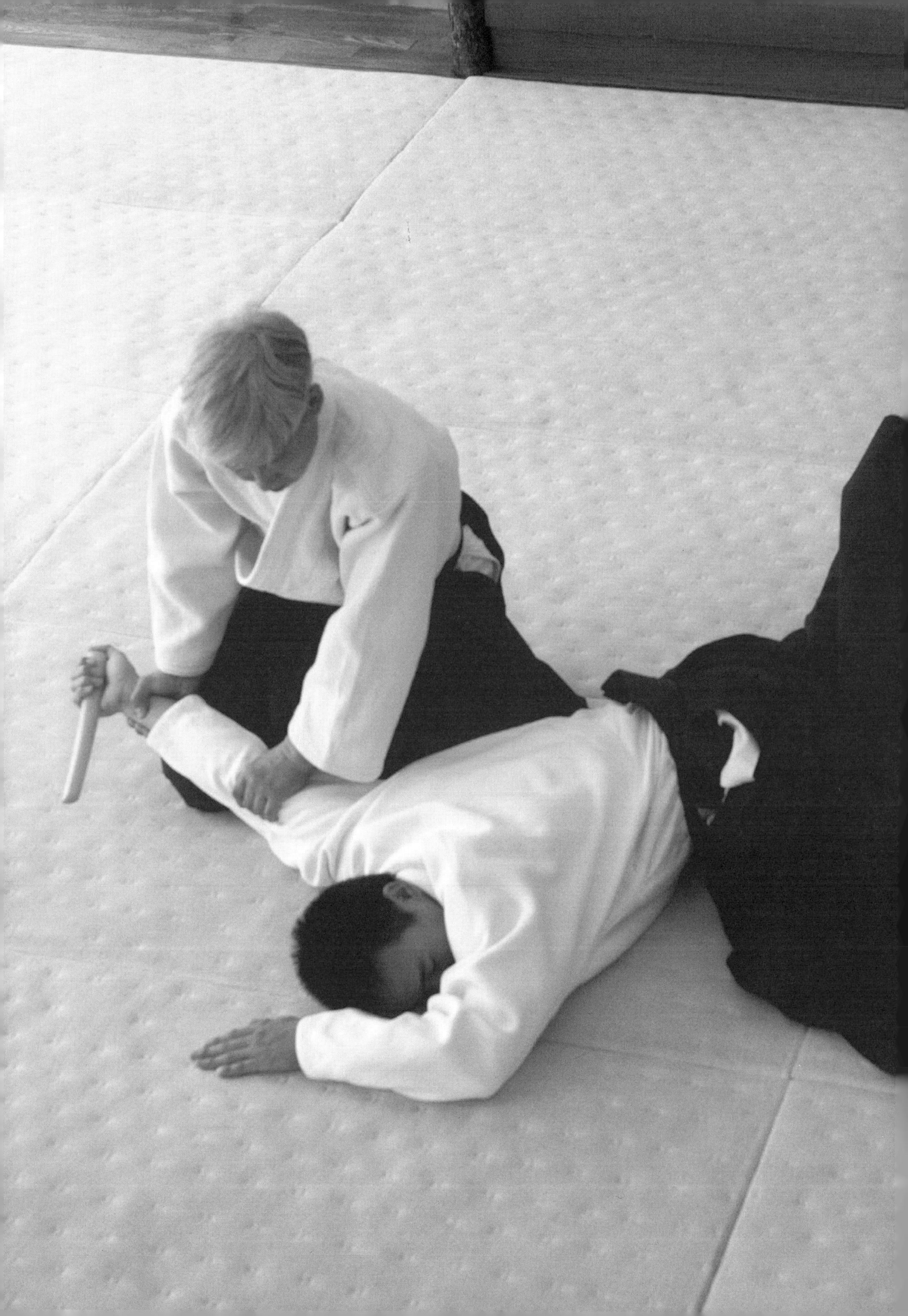

CHAPTER 5

Acquiring Skill in Applied Technique
Advanced Training Methods

NAGE-WAZA 1

MOROTE-DORI KOKYU-NAGE 1
Use your body flexibly and throw your partner dynamically

Maintain a steady flow of movement from the initial turn to the throw

In *kokyu-nage* techniques, the mind, technique, and body need to be unified; manifest the natural power thus generated through your hand-swords to throw your partner. In this version of *kokyu-nage*, from the initial turn to the final throw, your movement must be smooth and flowing.

Harmonize the turn, your partner's momentum, and the cutting down of your hand-sword, to throw your partner. Do not stiffen up but keep your entire body flexible and move dynamically.

1: In the *ai-hanmi* stance.

Draw your partner out to the front.

Do not let your partner break his grip, send him flying from his back foot.

4–6: While turning, *tori* cuts down to the front with a big step forward to throw *uke*.

> As illustrated in photos 3 and 4, harmonize your body movement and the cutting down of the sword in one smooth motion. Draw your partner out to the front, harmonize your foot movement with that flow, and cut down to throw him.

2–3: As soon as *uke* attempts to grab *tori*'s arm from the side, *tori* enters to *uke*'s outside while raising his hand-sword.

> Throw dynamically with your entire body.

NAGE-WAZA 2

MOROTE-DORI KOKYU-NAGE 2
Harmonize your body movement and the motion of your hand-swords

1: In the *ai-hanmi* stance.

2

Hand and foot should be facing the same direction.

5–6: *Tori* uses his hand-sword to cut down to *uke*'s inside while opening on his front foot, and leads *uke*.

Use your free hand-sword to cut in deeply to your partner's inside

The key point in this version of *kokyu-nage* is to make the entering, the sweeping turn, the entry to the inside of your partner, and the cutting down of the throw in one free flowing movement. Also, the free hand-sword that is placed under your partner's arms must extend under his elbows. If your partner's elbows are extended, he will be pointed to the front, the proper direction.

3–4: As soon as *uke* attempts to grab *tori*'s arm, *tori* enters to his outside while turning and raising his hand-sword.

As illustrated in photos 3–6, the entering, turn, and opening of the body movements should be harmonized with the motion of the hand-swords in a free flow.

POINT: Make sure your free hand-sword is extended out under your partner's elbow and to his inside when you throw him.

7: The free hand-sword should control your partner's elbow from underneath.

8–9: *Tori* takes a big step in to throw *uke*.

153

NAGE-WAZA 3

MOROTE-DORI JUJI-GARAMI
Cross your partner's arm and lock his elbows to throw him

1: In the *ai-hanmi* stance.

2–4: As soon as *uke* attempts to grab *tori*'s arm, *tori* enters to *uke*'s outside while turning and raising his hand-sword.

5–6: *Tori* opens up on his front foot while crossing *uke*'s arms.

POINT: Use your corresponding hands to cross partner's arms to break his posture.

1

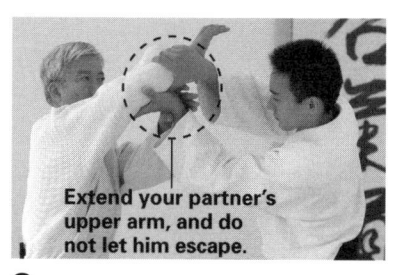

2: Grab your partner's lower wrist so he cannot escape.

Extend your partner's upper arm, and do not let him escape.

3: Use your upper hand to grab your partner's upper wrist while cutting down with both hands.

Pull back on your partner's top arm

In this *morote-dori juji-garami* technique, the key is to cross your partner's arms, thereby controlling his elbows, and throwing him. Use left hand on left, right hand on right (or vice-versa) to break his posture. In order to form a good cross with your partner's arms, use your top hand to bring his arm to the outside; then it will be possible to break his posture.

As illustrated in photos 3–6, the entering, turn, and opening of the body movements should be harmonized with the motion of the hand-swords in a free flow.

7–9: *Tori* applies the cross armlock, steps in, and throws *uke*.

4: Cut down to the outside with the upper hand.

As in photos 3–4, cut to the outside with your upper arm. Do this far enough to form a cross with your partner's elbows, as in photo 5.

5: Lock his elbows in a well-formed cross, and throw him.

NAGE-WAZA 4

USHIRO RYOTEKUBI-DORI KOKYU-NAGE
Use your hand-swords to raise your partner up as if placing him on your back

1: In the *ai-hanmi* stance.

2–3: *Uke* cuts down on *tori*'s arm and attempts to grab *tori*'s wrists from behind.

5: *Tori* takes a big step forward while cutting down with his hand-swords and throws *uke*.

Use your power to draw your partner out to the front

In this *ushiro ryotekubi-dori kokyu-nage* technique, you raise your hand-swords and then cut down to throw your partner, who is holding your wrists from behind. You have to use your power to draw him to the front. Raise your hand-swords as if placing him on your back and, from that position, cut down and throw him smoothly to the front.

4: *Tori* raises his hand-swords as soon as *uke* tries to grab.

POINT: When you cut down with your hand-swords, make sure that your partner is on his toes, almost riding on your back. Use that momentum to draw him out and bring him forward.

After bringing your partner up, cut down to the front; when you throw him, do not pull your arms in, or else you will break the flow of the technique.

NAGE-WAZA 5

KATA-DORI SHOMEN-UCHI SHIHO-NAGE
Keep your hips low to move under your partner's arm, and throw

1: In the *ai-hanmi* stance.

2: *Uke* grabs *tori*'s shoulder.

3: *Tori* enters while delivering a neutralizing strike to *uke*'s face, who moves to block it.

7–8: *Tori* cuts down and throws *uke*.

9

POINT: Enter low under your partner's arms.

1: Your knees must be bent and your hips low.

Keep your feet and hips flexible when you make the low turn, and be sure your hips have moved all the way around.

2: Keep your hand-sword against your forehead as you step in.

Keep your feet and hips flexible while entering from a low position

In this *kata-dori shomen-uchi shiho-nage* technique, your partner has grabbed your shoulder and attacks with *shomen*. You step under his arms, turn, and cut down, throwing him in *shiho-nage*. The key point here is to keep your hips well under his arm, down low, and maintain flexibility in your feet and hips. Do not stiffen up when you enter or your balance will be broken.

4–5: While turning, *tori* cuts down *uke*'s arm, leads him, and controls his wrist.

6: While keeping his center of gravity low, *tori* steps in and turns, raising both hand-swords.

POINT: Enter low under your partner's arms.
Keep your feet and hips flexible when you make the low turn, and be sure your hips have moved all the way around.

10

Your partner must retain his grip of your shoulder until just prior to the throw. Your partner lets go of your shoulder when he is fully turned and ready to take a breakfall. If he does not let go it will be difficult to fall.

3: Step all the way in under your partner's arms.

4: The turn.

5: Cut down with both hand-swords and throw.

KATAME-WAZA 1

KATA-DORI SHOMEN-UCHI DAI-NIKYO (OMOTE)
From the initial strike to the turn, keep your hand-sword in contact with the hand-sword of your partner

1: In the *ai-hanmi* stance.

2: *Uke* grabs *tori*'s shoulder.

3: *Tori* enters to *uke*'s outside while striking his face; *uke* blocks that strike.

7–8: *Tori* applies the dai-nikyo lock to *uke*'s left wrist, and controls the right elbow.

POINT: Keep your hand-sword in contact with that of your partner from the neutralizing strike to the turn.

1: Strike while entering, and your partner blocks.

2: While turning, maintain contact with your partner's hand-sword.

Your partner harmonizes with your movement, and makes a step in.

160

Both partners should keep their hand-swords in contact

In this technique, when your partner grabs your shoulder, you enter while striking his face, and then, while making a sweeping turn, cut down and pin him by controlling his wrist and elbow.

The hand-sword that strikes your partner's face should then remain in contact with his hand-sword during the turn and until the control of his wrist and elbow. Failure to do this means you will have to apply a different technique, so you will not be able to practice this one. Also, your partner should harmonize with your big sweeping turn and the move in, while maintaining contact with your hand-sword.

4–6: While turning, *tori* cuts down with a right step backward.

9–11: *Tori* steps in while cutting down on *uke*'s left arm and applying the *dai-nikyo* lock, bringing *uke* face down to the ground. *Tori* binds *uke*'s shoulder and arm, and pins him.

3: Enter while controlling your partner's elbow and wrist (and applying *atemi*).

4: Fully control your partner's elbow and wrist.

KATAME-WAZA 2

KATA-DORI SHOMEN-UCHI DAI-NIKYO (URA)
At the instant you face your partner apply the *dai-nikyo* lock

> Your partner takes one step forward while maintaining contact with your hand-sword.

1: In the *gyaku-hanmi* stance.

2: *Uke* grabs *tori*'s shoulder.

3: *Tori* enters while striking *uke*'s face, and *uke* blocks that neutralizing attack.

> In applying the *dai-nikyo* lock, lead your partner so he faces you, as in photo 9.

7: *Tori* enters on his front foot while controlling *uke*'s elbow and wrist.

8–10: While turning, *tori* cuts down on *uke*'s arm while leading *uke* into the *dai-nikyo* lock against his shoulder, and by dropping his hips.

Always bring your partner round to face you

In this technique, lead your partner while making a sweeping turn and cutting down; enter again, and turn once more while applying the *dai-nikyo* lock. Break his posture and pin him. In all of the *dai-nikyo* techniques, it is important to apply the lock as soon as you face your partner.

Your partner should follow your movement and end up facing you. If your partner stops your movement at the stage of photo 8, apply an elbow lock technique.

4–6: While turning, *tori* cuts down with his hand-sword and leads *uke*.

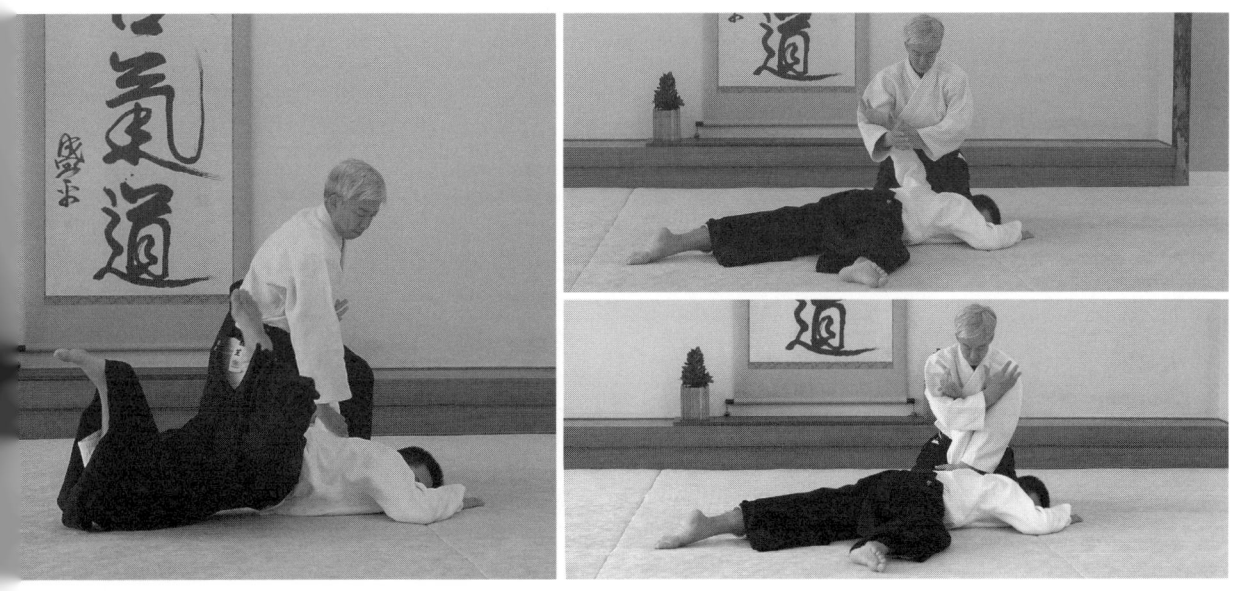

11–13: *Tori* brings *uke* down to the mat, and pins him.

KATAME-WAZA 3

USHIRO RYOKATA-DORI DAI-SANKYO (OMOTE)
Lower your hips, and slide under your partner's arms

1: In the *ai-hanmi* stance.

2–3: *Uke* cuts down on *tori*'s arm and then moves around to grab *tori*'s shoulders from behind.

> When you shift your grip, do not relax and do not stop applying pressure.

7–8: With the *dai-sankyo* lock in place and while controlling *uke*'s elbow, *tori* turns and steps back, pulling *uke* down.

9–11: *Tori* brings *uke* face down to the mat, and pins him.

Slide under your partner's arms and apply the *dai-sankyo* lock

In this technique, your partner grabs both of your shoulders from behind. In this case, you apply the *omote dai-sankyo* lock to his wrist after lowering your hips and sliding under his arms, and then turn with a step back to break his posture to bring him down in a pin.

The key point here is to lower your hips and slide under your partner's arms to apply the *dai-sankyo* lock, and then to apply pressure all the way to the pin.

Lower your hips while sliding under your partner's arms.

4: *Tori* raises both hand-swords and then lowers his hips while sliding under *uke*'s arms with a step back on his front foot; *tori* prepares to apply the *dai-sankyo* lock.

5–6: *Tori* applies *atemi* to the face of *uke*.

POINT: Do not use just your hand, but employ *atemi* while applying the *dai-sankyo* lock.

KATAME-WAZA 4

USHIRO RYOKATA-DORI DAI-SANKYO (URA)
Lower your hips, slide to the back, and apply the *dai-sankyo* (*ura*) lock to your partner's wrist

1: In the *ai-hanmi* stance.

2–3: *Uke* cuts down on *tori*'s arm and then grabs *tori*'s shoulders from behind.

Apply the *dai-sankyo* lock to your partner's wrist from his side.

6–9: *Tori* turns on the back foot while entering to *uke*'s side, and then turns again to break *uke*'s posture.

Apply the *dai-sankyo* lock to your partner's outside

This *ura* technique follows the same pattern as the previous example: lower your hips to enter to the back and apply the *dai-sankyo* lock. Here, however, an extra turn is added while controlling and pinning *uke*. When you bend under your partner's arms be sure to not lose your balance. Also, keep the locking pressure on your partner's arm throughout.

Lower your hips and slide under your partner's arms.

4: *Tori* raises his arms and then lowers his hips as he steps back on his front foot, then applies the *dai-sankyo* lock to *uke*'s wrist,

5: *Tori* applies *atemi* as he enters to *uke*'s side.

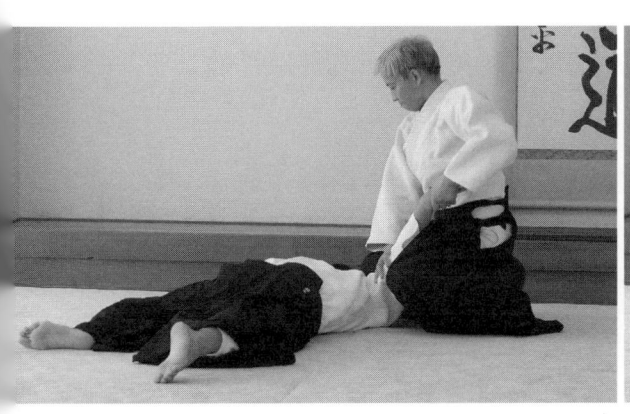

10–11: *Tori* brings *uke* face down to the mat, switches his grip, and pins *uke*.

NAGE-KATAME-WAZA 1
MOROTE-DORI KOTE-GAESHI
Harmonize the raising of your hand-swords, the cutting down, and your body movement, to apply the technique

1: In the *ai-hanmi* stance.

2–3: *Uke* attempts to grab *tori*'s arm with both his hands.

4: *Tori* enters to *uke*'s outside while raising his hand-sword.

As illustrated in photos 4–6, harmonize your hand-sword and body movement as you enter, turn, and cut up and down. As illustrated in photo 6, your partner's posture should be completely broken.

5

8–11: *Tori* steps in and applies *kote-gaeshi* to throw *uke*.

Harmonize the motion of your hand-swords and your body movement, and use your whole body to break your partner's posture

The *kote-gaeshi* techniques are the primary throw-and-pin techniques. You lock your partner's wrist, turn it to throw, and then pin. In all of the *kote-gaeshi* techniques, you must use more than just your hands—you need to harmonize the entry, the turn; indeed, all of the movements, to break his posture and throw your partner.

In this *morote-dori kote-gaeshi* technique, harmonize the motion of your hand-swords and the body movement, and break your partner's posture with your entire body. In this technique, in which you are held by both hands on one arm, the *ma-ai* is close, so you must make all of your movements in one smooth flow to avoid getting tangled with your partner.

As illustrated in photos 5–7, enter to your partner's outside while turning to lead him. Do this in one flowing movement without stopping.

6: While pulling back on his front foot, *tori* cuts down on *uke*'s arm and applies the *kote-gaeshi* lock.

7: *Tori* turns to lead *uke*.

12–13: *Tori* brings *uke* face down to the mat and pins him.

NAGE-KATAME-WAZA 2

USHIRO RYOTEKUBI-DORI KOTE-GAESHI
Do not break the flow of your partner's movement while you move

1: In the *ai-hanmi* stance.

2–3: *Uke* cuts down on *tori*'s arm, and then grabs *tori*'s wrists from behind.

5–7: *Tori* steps forward with the front foot, applies the *kote-gaeshi* to *uke*'s wrist while turning, and leads him.

8–10: *Tori* opens to his inside and throws *uke* with *kote-gaeshi*.

Harmonize the motion of your hand-swords and the turn

Here is a *kote-gaeshi* lock, throw, and pin used when your partner grabs your wrists from behind. You take one step forward on the front foot while raising both hand-swords, and then turn to lead your partner; open to the side to throw him. It is important to do all of this in one flowing movement. Throughout this technique, harmonize all the movements.

> If your partner pulls his hips back, you cannot train correctly in this technique. Use his body completely, and he should follow.

4

> As illustrated in photos 4–6, harmonize your hand-sword and body movement as you enter, turn, and cut up and down. As illustrated in photo 6, your partner's posture should be completely broken.

11–12: *Tori* brings *uke* to the mat while controlling his elbow, and pins him.

171

TANTO-DORI 1
TANTO-DORI YOKOMEN-UCHI DAI-GOKYO (OMOTE)
In *dai-gokyo*, control your partner's wrists from above

1: In the *ai-hanmi* stance.

2–3: As soon as *uke* makes a *yokomen* knife strike, *tori* enters deeply to *uke*'s outside while controlling *uke*'s attacking arm and simultaneously applying *atemi*.

4–5: *Tori* applies the *dai-gokyo* lock to *uke*'s wrist while controlling his elbow.

9: *Tori* presses his inner knee against *uke*'s ribs and extends his arm.

10: *Tori* raises *uke*'s arm and wrist at a right angle to the mat and applies pressure to *uke*'s wrist.

Use your entire body to apply pressure to your partner's wrist, and his palm will naturally open

In Aikido, we have various techniques against armed attacks such as a knife, jo, and so on.

Here we will introduce *dai-gokyo* knife-taking techniques against a *yokomen* strike.

The key points are:
—Enter deeply to break your partner's posture when he makes a *yokomen* knife attack.
—Do not control your partner's wrist joint from underneath but from above. If you try to take it from underneath the knife will cut your own wrist.
—When you take the knife, place his wrist and elbow at a right angle, press down on his wrist, and he will naturally open his palm.

6–8: *Tori* cuts down on *uke*'s wrist to bring him down to the mat.

11: *Tori* uses his entire body to apply pressure to *uke*'s wrist, making him release his grip on the knife, which *tori* takes.

173

TANTO-DORI 1 (Continued)

POINT 1: Enter deeply to control your partner's *yokomen* strike.
Enter deeply against the attack, your outer hand-sword controlling the strike and your inner hand-sword applying *atemi*. Be sure to enter deeply enough to break your partner's posture completely and thus control the *yokomen* attack.

Enter with *atemi*.

With a deep entry and your hand-swords, control your partner's *yokomen* knife attack.

POINT 2: Grab his wrist joint from above.
When you apply the *dai-gokyo* lock, do not bend your partner's arm as you grasp his wrist joint. Note the difference between this lock and *dai-ikkyo*.

Lock his wrist from above.

POINT 3: Pin your partner's arm at a right angle and take the knife.
After bringing your partner face down on the mat, press your inner knee against his ribs, and extend his arm. Then, raise his arm in a right angle with the elbow and the wrist, and use your entire body to place pressure on his wrist joint. Your partner will naturally release his grip, making it possible to take the knife.

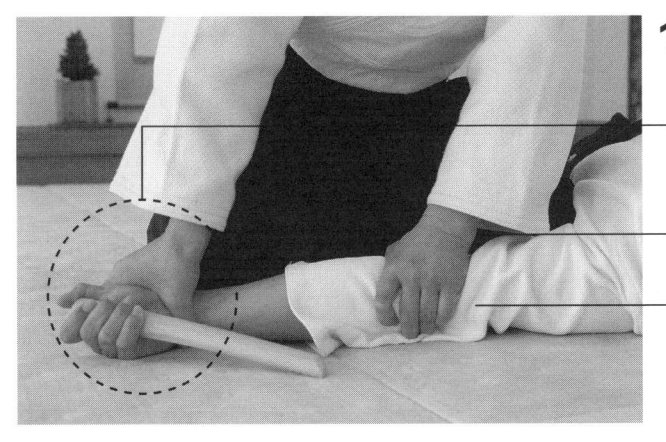

1

Press your front knee against his wrist, and use the base of your index finger to apply pressure.

Press your inner knee against your partner's ribs.

Extend your partner's arm.

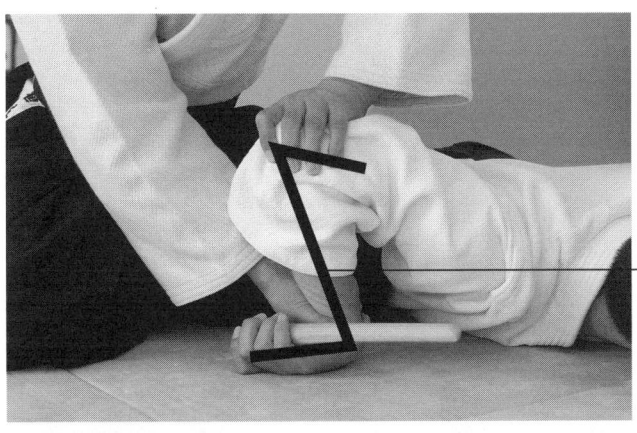

2

As illustrated in photos 1 and 2, move your partner's wrist joint into this position.

Place your partner's arm and wrist at a right angle to the mat while applying pressure to his wrist joint. Make sure the angle of the pin is complete; if the angle is too shallow the pin will not be effective.

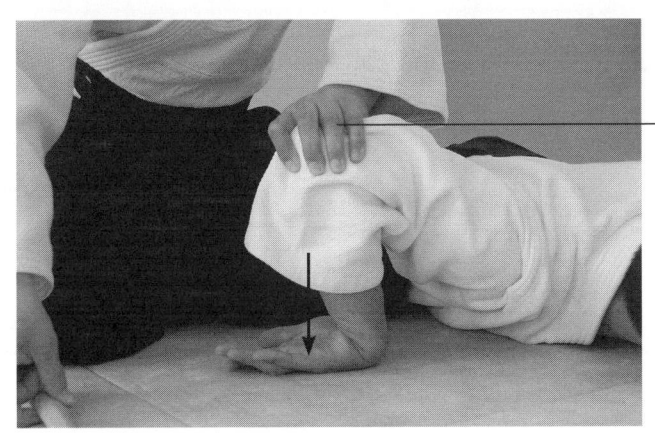

3

Keep your partner's wrist straight while applying pressure with your entire body.

Keep applying pressure until your partner naturally opens his palm and you can take the knife.

TANTO-DORI 2

TANTO-DORI YOKOMEN-UCHI DAI-GOKYO (URA)
Control your partner's wrist from above and turn

> Pay attention to the direction of the blade when you move, taking care not to injure yourself.

> Grab your partner's wrist from above.

1: In the *ai-hanmi* stance.

2: As soon as *uke* makes a *yokomen* knife attack, *tori* enters deeply to *uke*'s outside.

3: Tori controls *uke*'s attacking arm with his front hand-sword while applying *atemi* with his back hand-sword; *tori* then applies *dai-gokyo*.

4–7: While controlling *uke*'s elbow, *tori* spins and cuts down on *uke*'s arm.

8: *Tori* brings *uke* face down to the mat.

9: *Tori* presses his inside knee against *uke*'s ribs and extends *uke*'s arm.

Pay attention to the direction of the blade when you move

As in the previous technique, control your partner's *yokomen* knife attack with the *dai-gokyo* lock, but here use a turn to break his posture and pin him face down. While applying the *dai-gokyo* lock and turning, be careful of the direction of the blade, making sure you do not allow yourself to be cut.

10: *Tori* places *uke*'s elbow and wrist at a right angle, and applys pressure.

11: *Tori* continues to apply pressure with his entire body on *uke*'s wrist, then takes the knife.

177

TANTO-DORI 3

TANTO-DORI TSUKI-HIJI-GIME
Turn your partner's wrist while keeping his arm close to your body

1: In the *ai-hanmi* stance.

2: As soon as *uke* thrusts with the knife, *tori* enters to *uke*'s outside while controlling his arm.

5: *Tori* brings *uke*'s arm close against his body.

6–7: *Tori* applies the lock to *uke*'s elbow, and pins.

POINT: Keep your partner's elbow close against your body. From the control of the thrust to the final pin the flowing movement is:

1: Enter to avoid the thrust while controlling your partner's wrist.
2: Turn his wrist while keeping it close against your body.
3: Wrap your arms against your side to pin him.

When you lock your partner's wrist, keep his arm close against your body.

Slide your hand-sword along the arm to his wrist.

1: Pay attention to the entry of your back foot; make sure it is deep enough to completely avoid your partner's line of attack.

2: Slide your controlling hand-sword along your partner's arm to grab his wrist.

When you enter, pull back on your back foot

As soon as your partner makes a knife thrust, enter while controlling his wrist; turn his arm inward against your body while applying a lock to his elbow, and take away the knife.

The key point here is to move decisively. Enter deeply while controlling your partner's wrist, pull him down while extending his arm, and apply the lock to his elbow. Do all this in one flowing movement. When you apply the lock to your partner's elbow, wrap both your arms around his elbow, and keep it close to your body.

3–4: *Tori* grabs *uke*'s wrist and twists it down.

8: *Tori* takes the knife from *uke*.

3: Pull your partner forward while turning his wrist and bring his arm against your body.

4: Keep your partner's body tight against your body.

> Use both of your arms to wrap his elbow against your side.
>
> Extend his arm against his side, and keep the angle big.

TANTO-DORI 4

TANTO-DORI TSUKI-KOTE-GAESHI
Pin your partner's wrist and shoulder, be careful of the blade, and take away the knife

Pull the back foot out of the way.

1: In the *ai-hanmi* stance.

2: As soon as *uke* thrusts with the knife, *tori* enters to his outside while controlling *uke*'s attacking arm with his front hand-sword.

Throw him in front of you.

6–8: *Tori* turns in and throws *uke*.

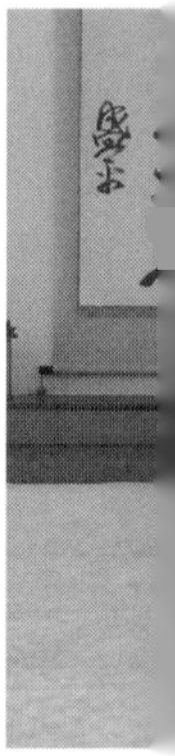

9–11: *Tori* brings *uke* face down to the mat, pins *uke*'s wrist joint, and takes away the knife.

Turn the blade toward your partner's face when you apply *kote-gaeshi*

This technique is used against a knife thrust. Enter directly to your partner's outside when he thrusts, throw him with *kote-gaeshi*, pin him face down, apply a jointlock, and take away the knife.

Points to watch: When you apply the *kote-gaeshi* throw, make sure the blade is pointed in the direction of your partner's face. Also, do not try to throw your partner outward and away from you. It is important to throw him in front of you.

Enter directly to your partner's outside when he thrusts.

Point the knife in the direction of your partner's face.

3: *Tori* slides his hand down *uke*'s arm to *uke*'s wrist.

4: *Tori* turns and leads *uke*.

5: *Tori* applies *kote-gaeshi* to *uke*'s wrist, keeping the knife turned in the direction of *uke*'s face.

POINT: How to take away the knife
When you take away the knife, keep your partner's elbow and wrist bent as you pin him face down on the mat. Keep the pressure on his arm with your knee, lock his wrist and shoulder, loosen his grip, and take away the knife.

1: As you turn your partner face down, bend his wrist and elbow strongly in the same direction.

2: Use your knee to pin your partner's arm and apply pressure with your entire body against his wrist joint and shoulder.

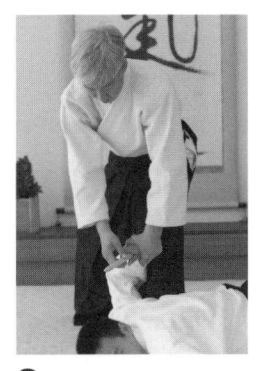

3: Keep the pressure on your partner's wrist until he loosens his grip, and then take away the knife.

FUTARI-DORI 1

FUTARI-DORI 1
Make full use of your hand-swords to lead your partners as one and then throw them

1: In the *ai-hanmi* stance.

2–4: When the two *uke* grab *tori*'s arms from the sides, *tori* takes a step forward on his front foot while raising his hand-swords.

5–6: *Tori* turns, bringing the two *uke* together.

7–8: *Tori* cuts down with his hand-swords, and throws both *uke*.

Make both partners move in one direct line

This is a technique to use when attacked by two partners. It is not a technique for beginners, but is part of the advanced Aikido repertoire that I would like to introduce here.

It is important to move both partners as one, making them come together. In order to do that, you must enter deeply while making full use of your hand-swords to break your partners' postures. While turning, use your hand-swords to keep them in close contact, bring them together in one direct line, and it will be easy to throw them.

POINT: Make full use of your hand-swords to bring your partners together.
Turn while using the hand-swords, bringing your partners together, and throw.
Photos 2–7 from a different angle.

1: Your partners grab your arms from the side.

2–3: Raise your hand-swords while staying centered, and enter.

Pull your partners' arms in your direction.
Pull here.
Step back.

4: Turn to face the same direction as your partners.

5–6: After the turn, bring both hand-swords up, and bring your partners together.

FUTARI-DORI 2

FUTARI-DORI 2
Use the contact of your hand-swords and body movement to bring your partners together

1

2

> Bring your upper hand-sword around.

> Pull in with the lower hand-sword.

5: *Tori* steps forward on his front foot while raising his hand-swords.

6: While turning, *tori* brings the upper hand around to bring the *uke* together.

7

> Use your upper hand-sword to bring your partner around while using the lower hand-sword to turn; do this in harmony to bring your partners together.

Harmonize the turn and the movement of your hand-swords

In this technique, one partner holds your wrist with both of his hands, while the other partner holds your wrist while applying a choke hold from behind. You must use the contact of your hand-swords and the body movement of the turn to bring them together, and then throw.

The key point here is to turn while smoothly moving the hand-swords to bring your partners together. Also, as soon as your partner attempts the choke hold, pull your chin in.

3: One *uke* grabs *tori*'s arm with both his hands while the other *uke* grabs *tori*'s wrist and attempts a choke hold from behind.

4: As soon as *uke* attempts the choke hold, *tori* pulls his chin in.

8–9: *Tori* cuts down with both hand-swords to throw *uke*.

合氣
盛平

CHAPTER 6

Aikido Training Procedures

REI-HO 1
REI (Bowing with Respect)

Bend from your hips to lower your body forward
During training, we bow to the *shomen*, to the instructor, and to our partners. When you bow, be sure to keep your neck and back straight. Bow forward from the hips with your collar and neck in a straight line.

REI

1: Keep your back straight and your hands rested lightly on your thighs as you sit in *seiza*.

2: Place your hands on the mat.

3: Bow forward from the hips.

4: Return to the *seiza* position.

REI to the Shomen

1: Face the front of the *dojo* in *seiza*.

2: Bow to the *shomen*. Do this upon entering and leaving the *dojo*.

REI to your partner

1: Face each other in *seiza*.

2: Bow to each other with respect. Do this at the beginning and end of training.

Do not look straight down, rather keep your partner within your field of vision.

REI-HO 2
FORMALLY STANDING AND SITTING

When you stand, do so from the left foot; when you sit, do so from the right foot

In Aikido, we have a set pattern of standing and sitting. At all times, the movement should be smooth and unforced. When you stand, rise up on the left foot, and when you sit, pull back on the right foot.

How to Stand

1: In *seiza*.

2: Rise up on your toes.

Sit up on the toes.

3: Step forward on your left knee, and stand.

4: Stand straight up in one movement.

How to Sit

1

2: Step back on your right foot.

3: Bring your right knee to the mat.

Drop your hips straight down and end up on your toes.

4: Bring your left knee down as well, and sit on your toes.

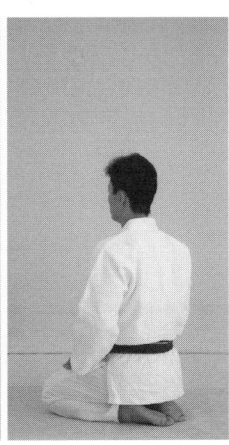

5: Settle down into *seiza*.

WRIST WARM-UP EXERCISES

kote-mawashi warm-up

1: Place your left thumb against the base of your right thumb, and the left little finger against the base of your right little finger, with your open palms.

Do not raise your elbows.

Keep your arms against your sides, and harmonize the power of both hands to give your wrist a good stretch.

2–3: While harmonizing the movements with inhaling and exhaling, bend your arms in, giving your wrist a good stretch. Always do this exercise on both sides.

Keep your wrists flexible while learning how to apply the lock
In Aikido we have many techniques that lock and pin the joints. Prior to actual training, it is necessary to stretch the joints. Also, these warm-up exercises teach you how to correctly apply the locks in practice. Here, we have the *kote-mawashi* warm-up and the *kote-gaeshi* warm-up.

Kote-gaeshi warm-up

1: Hold your left thumb in front of your chest while holding the base of your right ring finger: the other fingers of your left hand should be held against the base of your right thumb, wrapping up your right palm.

Do not raise your elbows.

While bending your wrist, keep your movement centered up and down.

2–3: Using the power of both arms, turn your wrist in while pulling down. Do this on both sides.

SHIHO-NAGE BACK STRETCH EXERCISE
Bend the knees and stretch the entire body

Shiho-nage back stretch exercise (omote)

1

2: *Uke* grabs *tori*'s wrists (they should be in *ai-hanmi*).

3–4: *Tori* raises both hand-swords while turning.

Shiho-nage back stretch exercise (ura)

1

2: *Uke* grabs *tori*'s wrists (in the *ura* technique, they should be in *gyaku-hanmi*).

3–4: *Tori* enters to *uke*'s outside and starts to turn.

Do not just dangle your partner.

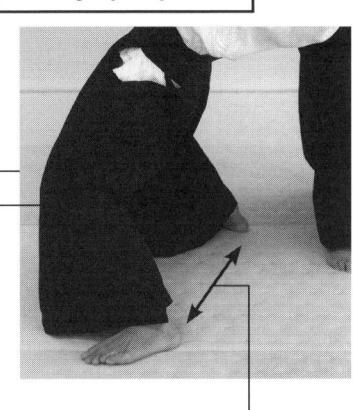

Do not twist your hips.

5: *Tori* cuts down half-way with both hand-swords to stretch *uke*'s back.

Bend your knees and fully stretch your back.

In this exercise, remain in *hanmi*, but bring your legs in line with your shoulders.

Do not just dangle him.

5: *Tori* raises both hand-swords while turning.

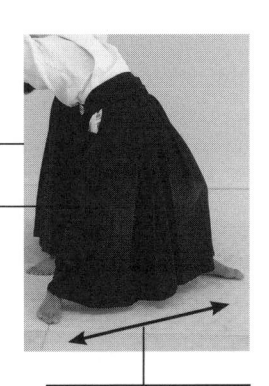

6: *Tori* cuts down half-way with both hand-swords to stretch *uke*'s back.

Keep your feet in a straight line, the width of your shoulders.

Do not twist your hips.

The knees are bent and the back is fully stretched.

AFTER TRAINING STRETCH

Let your partner grab your wrists. While raising your hand-swords, turn and stretch your partner across your back. Lift him off his feet, to give his back a good stretch, making sure he has a tight grip on your wrists. This is a good post-training exercise.

TRAINING ATTIRE

Always keep your training uniform clean for practice

If you have the proper attire, your training will be in good order. This is the first step in the practice of Aikido.

Be careful:
—To tie your belt to the side.
—Not to wear your *hakama* too long so it drags on the mat
—To keep your uniform clean.

Examples of Proper Training Wear

Select the right size uniform for you. It is prohibited to wear a uniform that is too tight or too big across the chest.

Keep your fingernails and toenails cut short.

Female practitioners should not have the clothing covering the chest open. It is fine to wear long white training pants underneath.

The *hakama* should not be long enough to drag on the mat.

How to Tie the Belt

Good example: Tie the belt horizontally.

Bad example: Do not tie the belt vertically.

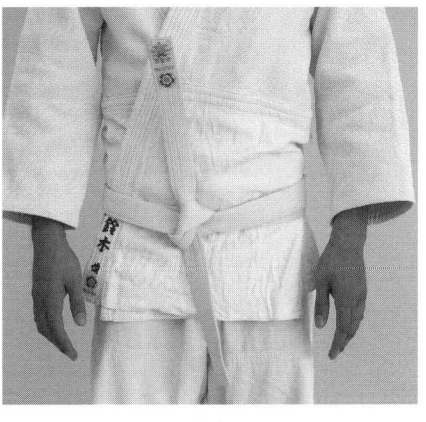

○   ×

Culture in International Construction

Despite the wide range of technologies involved, the construction industry still relies very heavily on people. Clients, managers, designers, investors and a whole host of other stakeholders are all involved in a crucial series of relationships that may be more important for project success than technical know-how. As construction projects become increasingly international, as well as interdisciplinary, the risks and costs of disharmonious working become ever larger. The growth of IT and the increased occurrences of mergers and joint ventures have created new problems, which require new solutions.

Recent research has generated profound insights into international differences in business culture. This new work presents up-to-date theory and practical guidance, identifying situations in which cultural differences present challenges. A focus on 'critical incidents', demonstrated in a range of case studies, will help readers to foresee situations in their own projects and processes, and so improve strategic and operational decision-making in construction collaborations. Detailed examples are taken from the Netherlands, Germany, Poland, Turkey, the UAE and China to explore a variety of problems in very different economic and cultural surroundings.

A range of professionals (contractors, developers, investors, architects, engineers, governments and public/private clients) will find this book highly valuable, as will researchers and students.

Wilco Tijhuis is a construction professional and entrepreneur. After starting his career in international positions in construction and development, he founded his own company. He is also active as an Assistant Professor at the University of Twente in the Netherlands on a part-time basis, specializing in international construction processes. His main research interests are strategy, management and risk, procurement and culture in construction. He is a joint coordinator of the international platform CIB W112 'Culture in Construction'.

Richard Fellows is Professor of Construction Business Management at Loughborough University, UK. He has taught at a number of universities in the UK, Hong Kong, China and beyond. He is a founder and joint coordinator of the international platform CIB W112 'Culture in Construction'. His main research interests are economics, contracts, organization and project management, and culture in construction.

About CIB and about the series

CIB, the International Council for Research and Innovation in Building and Construction, was established in 1953 to stimulate and facilitate international cooperation and information exchange between governmental research institutes in the building and construction sector, with an emphasis on those institutes engaged in technical fields of research.

CIB has since developed into a worldwide network of over 5000 experts from about 500 member organisations active in the research community, in industry or in education, who cooperate and exchange information in over 50 CIB Commissions and Task Groups covering all fields in building and construction related research and innovation.

http://www.cibworld.nl/

This series consists of a careful selection of state-of-the-art reports and conference proceedings from CIB activities.

Open & Industrialized Building A. *Sarja*
ISBN: 9780419238409. Published: 1998

Building Education and Research J. *Yang* et al.
ISBN: 978041923800X. Published: 1998

Dispute Resolution and Conflict Management P. *Fenn* et al.
ISBN: 9780419237003. Published: 1998

Profitable Partnering in Construction S. *Ogunlana*
ISBN: 9780419247602. Published: 1999

Case Studies in Post-Construction Liability A. *Lavers*
ISBN: 9780419245707. Published: 1999

Cost Modelling *M. Skitmore* et al.
(allied series: Foundation of the Built Environment)
ISBN: 9780419192301. Published: 1999

Procurement Systems *S. Rowlinson* et al.
ISBN: 9780419241000. Published: 1999

Residential Open Building *S. Kendall* et al.
ISBN: 9780419238301. Published: 1999

Innovation in Construction *A. Manseau* et al.
ISBN: 9780415254787. Published: 2001

Construction Safety Management Systems *S. Rowlinson*
ISBN: 9780415300630. Published: 2004

Response Control and Seismic Isolation of Buildings *M. Higashino* et al.
ISBN: 9780415366232. Published: 2006

Mediation in the Construction Industry *P. Brooker* et al.
ISBN: 9780415471753. Published: 2010

Green Buildings and the Law *J. Adshead*
ISBN: 9780415559263. Published: 2011

New Perspectives on Construction in Developing Countries *G. Ofori*
ISBN: 9780415585724. Published: 2012

Contemporary Issues in Construction in Developing Countries *G. Ofori*
ISBN: 9780415585716. Published: 2012

Culture in International Construction *W. Tijhuis* et al.
ISBN: 9780415472753. Published: 2012